To Lewis,

with thanks for everything
that made our stay in Cambridge
so wonderful — support,
hospitality, warmth —

Joe Kerman
x.99

Concerto Conversations

The Charles Eliot Norton Lectures

1997–98

JOSEPH KERMAN

Concerto Conversations

HARVARD UNIVERSITY PRESS

Cambridge, Massachusetts

London, England · 1999

Library of Congress Cataloging-in-Publication Data

Kerman, Joseph, 1924–
    Concerto conversations / Joseph Kerman.
        p.   cm.—(The Charles Eliot Norton lectures ; 1997–98)
    Includes bibliographical references and index.
    ISBN 0-674-15891-1 (alk. paper)
    1. Concerto.   I. Title.   II. Series : Charles Eliot Norton
lectures ; 1997–1998.
ML1263.K47   1999
784.2'3—dc21   99-30919

To

Peter, Sharon,

and Tony

Contents

Concerto Conversations

Getting Started

"Concerto Conversations": that is one of those *double entendre* titles. I chose it because, first of all, so many of the concertos I love the most depend on musical conversation—or, better, because they make so much out of musical conversation. As will become evident. There was also another reason, and that was to dampen expectations which may well be raised by the majesty of the Charles Eliot Norton Lectures. Weighty things have been said under the aegis of this Chair, but anyone who may be looking for the present incumbent systematically to theorize the concerto, or illuminate its history, or develop a new aesthetic of the concerto will, I am afraid, be disappointed. My inclinations and my capabilities do not lie that way. These lectures will be more like conversations, sharing some of my observations about concertos, notions and intimations, enthusiasms and, I hope, insights.

As for the title "Getting Started," that emerged from a conversation with a friend who is a composer. Composers must inspire gratitude, respect, also some apprehension. In *Through the Looking Glass,* Tweedledee tells Alice, when she hears the Red King snoring, that he is dreaming about her, and that if he were to wake up she would "go out—bang!—just like a candle." Well, a musicologist is an Alice in some composer's dream. Therefore when I asked my friend if he would tell me about his experiences with a concerto he had recently written, I was far from just making conversation. I was attending to his every word. His brow furrowed. "The first problem," he confided, "is how to start the sucker." So if that is the first problem for the composer, I thought, it should be the first topic for our conversations.

·ↄ ·ↄ ·ↄ

Who, then, starts a concerto? The composer: or if that answer is too pat, the commissioning agency or patron. But who starts it when it's actually played and heard, at a concert?

My first concerto was when I was thirteen years old; we had seats, I remember, all the way up in the gods at the Albert Hall. Two men walked out onto the stage, and one of them I can still see, looking down from the heights: a very big man, with a very special gait. The other man is smaller, has a little beard, and carries a baton. Applause, a pause. The first man sits down at the piano and the other takes his place in front of the orchestra. Which one is going to play first?

You would not believe me if I said I remember asking myself that question: you would not believe me, and you would be right. But I do remember, will never forget, what happened next:

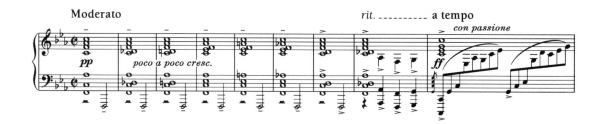

The music examples in this book—the rest of them are placed at the back—sometimes show the exact music referred to, as here, and sometimes provide merely cues or outlines for longer sections. Extended examples in music

notation are provided mainly for Lecture 6. At the lectures themselves, of course, sound recordings were used—and whenever practicable, videos, in this case a performance by Andrei Gavrilov with the New York Philharmonic under Vladimir Ashkenazy, filmed in Moscow.

To make my point I could have played a record made by Rachmaninoff himself, not so very long after he played in that memorable concert. I always preferred to use videos, however, as a way of bringing home the fact that concertos are viewed, witnessed as well as heard. Concertos not only bring dissimilar musical forces into play, they also enact scenes of human activity. Men and women and groups are brought into conjunction, cooperation, confrontation. Hence the common tendency to personify the solo and the orchestra in concertos—as conversationalists, as debaters, as antagonists, as Orpheus and the Furies.

What that child heard and saw and responded to was in fact a rather sophisticated means for getting started, rather unusual for a concerto. The solo instrument plays what is palpably an introduction to something else coming in the orchestra. I still feel that the introduction to Rachmaninoff's Second Piano Concerto (the conductor was Sir Henry Wood) is so impressive—nay, so shattering—that the obvious question "introduction to *what?*" hardly has time to register with an audience. The answer is a long melody played by the band, and I wish that this adult could feel entirely confident that the melody really holds up to its introduction. An individual is inherently more glamorous and attractive than a group, and given its head a solo instrument will tend to upstage an orchestra, like a child actor in the theater. Rachmaninoff avoids this, perhaps, by means of piano figuration during the orchestral melody that mostly churns away below, occasionally splashing over the top: a restless solo backdrop to the melody's morose orchestral sound and its almost surly affect. Rachmaninoff does the same thing near the beginning of his Third Piano Concerto.

Plate 1. Rachmaninoff, Piano Concerto No. 2:
Andrei Gavrilov with Vladimir Ashkenazy
and the Royal Philharmonic Orchestra

That anticlimax is a real danger in such situations is shown in what must be the longest of all solo introductions, by Camille Saint-Saëns in his Piano Concerto No. 2 in G minor. The opening ploy here is a rambling improvisational solo toccata in the style of Bach (or Bach-Busoni, or Bach-Siloti); during this the whispered question "introduction to *what*?" gets louder and louder, becomes clamorous, and toward the end threatens to muffle the piano entirely. The epigrammatic orchestral outburst that follows is loud enough, but does it have the requisite power, dignity, and distinction? Perhaps it makes sense in terms of the rest of the piece—starting with the next and rather surprising order of business, a piano nocturne—but whether in itself it justifies the long introduction is a real question.

Example 2

Anticlimax should not be an issue when a concerto introduction is played by the orchestra, introducing the solo. As a natural attention-grabber, a solo instrument thrives on promotion or boosts of any kind. The Chaikovsky[1] Violin Concerto begins with a quiet pair of orchestral phrases, bland and workaday in construction, harmony, rhythm, and all the rest. A drum roll, "action" music: this shoots up to a breathless fortissimo in just a few seconds and then subsides expectantly, just as quickly. Given the buildup it has received, the solo can now enter like a prima donna with a flourish, a pirouette, and a self-serving mini-cadenza before singing the aria that she was called in for in the first place, presumably. When the violin melody starts up, accompanied by pizzicato strings, like a big guitar, we feel we are right at home in the world of *Lucia di Lammermoor* and *Luisa Miller.*

Example 3

Making use of an introduction is, as I have already indicated, rather the exception as a launching-device. More common is the direct approach: bring the solo in right away with melody. The Schoenberg Piano Concerto is a beautiful example. Another is Beethoven's Piano Concerto No. 4 in G major. Shostakovich jump-starts both of his Cello Concertos in this manner.

Actually, it is more usual—more conventional—for the orchestra to acknowledge the solo by means of a discreet cough, before retiring to its stance as accompanist: as in the Mendelssohn Violin Concerto, or Bartók's Piano Concerto No. 3, or Rachmaninoff's Piano Concerto No. 3. Or a cough and a sigh, as in Benjamin Britten's Violin Concerto, Opus 15, from 1939. Three coughs and three sighs, actually.

Example 4

Presenting a tune up front to start a concerto is a sure way for the solo to make an impact, though obviously not the only way. The solo can establish itself more than adequately by simply laying down a special texture. The tune at the beginning of Ravel's Piano Concerto in G is in the piccolo, but the solo with its shimmering figuration could hardly ask for a more effective entrance. And the same can be said of the absolutely best-known of all concerto incipits, that of the Chaikovsky Piano Concerto. The piano chords that crash in after four bars may or may not constitute what is usually thought of as a texture, but they certainly introduce a marvelous sonority. One gets to the point where those invincible ringing chords block out, if they do not drown out, the great tune in the strings. In a stroke, Chaikovsky has given the piano an edge it will never lose throughout the whole of this relatively contentious composition.

Example 5

Example 6

Let me take a moment to make a number of small points about this familiar opening that I think may be instructive, though it's not certain they will all advance our conversation about getting started.

1. Chaikovsky found the chords (they are D-flat triads) in the midst of Liszt's Piano Concerto No. 2 in A major, at an important forceful passage marked Allegro deciso. The chords sweep up more brilliantly, twice as many in each bar. Where Liszt is ecstatic, or frenetic, depending on your point of view, Chaikovsky is majestic, spacing out the chords to let them ring better, and exploiting the instrument's range more powerfully.

2. Although that ringing piano sonority would have been impossible without the technology of Messrs. Steinway & Sons in the 1850s, it also owes a lot to a harmonic ploy by the composer that is as simple as it is potent. Starting out stressfully in a minor key, Chaikovsky dispels the cloud with a quick modulation moving to a bright new major key exactly when the piano enters.

3. The model for this complex was Liszt's other concerto, No. 1 in E-flat, where again the solo enters after an orchestral outburst that modulates at once to a new key. Liszt's piano does not accept this key; on the contrary, it switches back to the original key, the opposite of Chaikovsky's procedure. Instead of assenting, the solo here demurs, and when the modulation takes place it is to a new key mutually agreed upon (see Track 8, 0:23).

4. Those marvelous piano chords were a later revision. Originally Chaikovsky wrote them all rolled, or arpeggiated (the arpeggios are easily viewed in the Dover edition—which astonishingly gives no indication that they represent a discarded early version). Bless him for changing it.

5. Returning to the issue of anticlimax already raised in connection with Saint-Saëns and Rachmaninoff: especially after the revision, the sequel represents, in my apprehension, a letdown. When the tune is over and the piano replays it, with the chords transferred to pizzicato strings, the chords lack the éclat of the piano chords, obviously, and the twitchy *acciaccatura* rhythms in the piano more or less concede that fat piano chords are no match for a string orchestra when it comes to projecting effusive melody. The piano cuts its losses, fails to finish the tune, and drifts into a rather petulant cadenza instead.

In order to carry this passage off pianists often have recourse to heavy over-articulation, with a consequent loss of dignity that is regrettable, and probably irreversible. Tovey could have had this very place in mind when he inveighed against "the ordinary tendency [in piano concertos] to exploit the instrument in voluminous harmony which emulates the orchestra without achieving any character of its own."[2]

·⸱·⸱·⸱·

All the music mentioned up to this point has come from the nineteenth and early twentieth centuries. Composers in this era, the greatest era of the concerto, found endless other ways of getting started, as one hardly needs to say. Saint-Saëns, for example, a composer who would try anything, wrote ten concertos and several concerto-like shorter compositions, and not many of them introduce the solo instrument in the same way. Most orthodox is his Cello Concerto in A minor, one of his best works; this begins with a rhapsodic solo melody à la Mendelssohn, after a tiny orchestral preface that is less like a discreet cough than a starting gun. (The treatment of the tutti in the continuation smooths over a dull spot in the Mendelssohn, if one may say so without sacrilege.) Of the five piano concertos by Saint-Saëns, No. 2 has a long *solo* introduction to an *orchestral* theme, as already noted, whereas No. 3 has a long *orchestral* introduction to a *solo* theme, the introduction overlaid with a mysterious texture of piano arpeggios. No. 1 starts with a lengthy dialogue between piano and French horns *alla caccia* that is calculated to make Brahmsians cringe, and not only Brahmsians.

And Saint-Saëns' Piano Concerto No. 4 in C minor starts with a full-fledged orchestral melody—not with an orchestral introduction, like the Chaikovsky Violin Concerto and his own previous piano concerto, but with orchestral exposition of functional musical material. "Functional" is the key term here. The motifs of Chaikovsky's introduction drop out of the piece after they have done their advance work for the solo. Saint-Saëns' orchestral melody plays a major role in each of the work's two composite movements, generating formal variations in the first movement and serving as a sort of trio in the second.

Orchestral exposition of functional musical material: actually this is not all that common in nineteenth- and early twentieth-century concerto launchings, though every music lover will think of his or her favorites: Piano Concerto No. 1 by Edward MacDowell, No. 2 by Liszt, No. 3 by Prokofiev. I am disinclined to count the last two concertos discussed above in this category, as exposition of functional material by the orchestra. In Liszt No. 1, first of all, exposition is shared in the deepest sense between orchestra and solo; this a dialogue opening, a type that I shall return to in a later lecture. And the Chaikovsky is about piano sonority, not string melody. After the opening tune is heard two and a half times it disappears, notoriously, forever.

But one also thinks of Brahms: the Violin Concerto, the First Piano Concerto. Brahms, of course, does count; and of course Brahms was reviving the eighteenth-century concerto ritornello. So his concertos start with very substantial expository statements by the orchestra. Of all his many classicizing projects, this was perhaps the most extreme and the most obdurate; and the ritornello was not the only peculiarity of the early concerto that Brahms went back to, as we shall see. We need to have a look at opening orchestral ritornellos in early concertos, models for Brahms in the most general sense, and especially at solo entries in those concertos.

✦ ✦ ✦

Coming to the ritornello historically backwards in this way may have the effect of defamiliarizing something that musicians probably take too much for granted. Coldly considered, from a naive standpoint, if such a thing can be posited for a moment, the ritornello convention seems rather odd, and in its later manifestations even counterintuitive. In an age of instant gratification, it seems odd to leave the greatest plum, the solo instrument, waiting in the wings, stewing while the orchestra struts.

Still, the concerto in the eighteenth century certainly appears much more stable and unproblematic than in later times. The problems and the options that have been mooted in connection with nineteenth-century concertos, the uncertainties, the discretions and the indiscretions, the excitements and the dangers: all recede if they do not simply vanish. Vivaldi's brow never furrowed when he stared at that big white first page, with its staves preruled by a special five-nibbed pen, called a rastrum, by one of the musical girls at the Ospedale della Pietà in Venice. Vivaldi could compose an opera in five days. Vivaldi boasted that he could think up music faster than he could write it down. No doubt Mozart took longer, had to think harder. Yet Mozart as a concerto composer was closer to Vivaldi than to Saint-Saëns, and one reason is that for him, as for Vivaldi, the premise for getting started was a ritornello. The ritornello held fast to its function all through the global change in style and mood that occurred between the early and the late eighteenth century, through everything that separates Baroque music from Classical.

That function was never one of introduction. Neither the Classical nor the Baroque ritornello, for all their differences in style and form, sounds like a nineteenth-century orchestral introduction whipping up enthusiasm for the entrance of the solo instrument (as in the Chaikovsky Violin Concerto). While the ritornello unquestionably prepares the way for the solo, it does this by means of indispensable expository work of its own. It has further work to do on the architecture of the movement that it initiates; the word "ritornello," from *ritorno*, responds to the ritornello's basic agency in the form—to provide punctuation and closure. The ritornello or part of it needs to return at various points of the movement and at the end. This is true of Vivaldi and also of Mozart; it is still true with some modifications of Beethoven; and it is true again of Brahms.

As far as getting started is concerned, both at the actual start of the piece and also at the important, indeed crucial point where the orchestra stops and the solo enters, Vivaldi had no discernible problem. He had a highly efficient template for ritornellos and solo sections (which is not to say that Vivaldi holds scrupulously to these templates. If you write 900 concerto movements, template or not you will still produce a great number of exceptional pieces—and sure enough, there they are in your CD collection). The ritornello of a serious Baroque concerto is described in great detail—indeed, prescribed—in a much-cited treatise by Johann Joachim Quantz, one of many northerners, Bach being the most illustrious, who picked up on Vivaldi's practice (and also his facility: Quantz wrote over 300 concertos for flute). A concerto requires, says Quantz, "a magnificent ritornello at the beginning, which should be more harmonic than melodic, more serious than humorous, and relieved by unisons . . . There should be a pleasing and intelligible melody . . . the harmony changing, not with the eighth or quarter bars, but with half or full bars."[3] (Employing a slow harmonic rhythm, in today's language.) After which the solo enters with minimal accompaniment, displaying various facets of its capability and virtuosity.

In the Classical concerto, the solo does not enter after the ritornello with virtuoso display. It generally plays the first theme from the beginning of the ritornello. One means by which the ritornello has prepared for the solo has been by rehearsing that theme; when the solo plays it we attend less to the melody, which we already know, than to the new sonority. In particular, we hear and gauge the solo entry in reference to the opening of the ritornello. This may be called a *reciprocal* entry, as opposed to a *polar* entry as in Vivaldi. There are some wonderful exceptions among Mozart's thirty-odd concertos . . . and the Sinfonia Concertante for Violin and Viola, K. 365, which Charles Rosen has written about so luminously[4] . . . but the reciprocal solo entry is Mozart's rule.

Polarity and reciprocity can be seen in general terms as concerto principles, an idea I will develop later. Writing large-scale, impressive works that he would play himself at his benefit concerts, or *Akademien*, Mozart devised ritornellos that are three or four times as long as Vivaldi's, with a great variety of themes. Most beautiful of all is the last of the series, No. 27 in B-flat, K. 595, of 1791. The beginning of the ritornello is extraordinary in this piece, and the solo entry ordinary: almost too ordinary, suspiciously so. At the beginning, the one-bar preface in the lower strings—that quietly pulsing tonic chord before the violins play the first theme—gives the theme an aura unlike that of any other concerto of the time (and quite unlike the G-minor Symphony, despite the similarity in technical terms). This concerto starts not with a discreet cough or a sigh, but with an almost submusical rustle (Example 7a). Mozart's effect of mediation between musical sound and the sonic void has been repeated in such familiar later works as the Sibelius Violin Concerto and the First Violin Concerto by Prokofiev (Track 9).

Example 7

But the piano entrance of the theme in K. 595, predictably reciprocal, lacks the one-bar preface, lacks the aura. Though it does have a few added ornaments, the total effect is—dare I say weak? You might prefer to say *weich,* and perhaps Mozart would too: my German dictionary translates *weich* as "soft, tender, smooth, mellow, delicate," and only secondarily as "effeminate, weak." Mozart, with a new harmonic detail, deliberately softens this solo entry, makes it more *weich.* Beautifully sensitive to the variation, the original pointed woodwind fanfare responds by withdrawing to the quiet strings (Example 7b).

❦ ❦ ❦

Beethoven, I feel sure, would have said weak, *schwach.*

It is clear that from his earliest years (Beethoven wrote a piano concerto at age fourteen) this composer was uneasy with Classical concerto form, and not without cause. Accounts of his problems and innovations in this area abound in the Beethoven literature. The *Beethoven Compendium* of 1991 tells it differently than *The Beethoven Companion* of 1971, Robert Simpson contradicts Donald Tovey, and I will spare you my own version of what is by now a classic tale in musicology. Among other things, Beethoven resisted the idea of having the solo enter playing the first theme more or less as the orchestra had played it originally. Simple reciprocity at this point was too tame for him, too Classical.

The solo should make more of an effect—especially in piano concertos, where Beethoven was doing the playing himself. In Piano Concertos Nos. 1, 2, and 4 and in the juvenile effort, the reciprocal solo entry is evaded. In the Fifth Concerto it is transformed, and in the Third it is transcended. Let us listen to this latter work more closely: Beethoven's Piano Concerto No. 3 in C minor, Opus 37.

The C-minor Concerto opens with a quiet (but already tense) march-like theme that is later pressed into service as the ritornello's final cadential gesture. As such the theme is now presented fortissimo and in canon. Beethoven's original *cupo voce* becomes a rough, insistent shout [3.05].

Track 1

He had already done something of this kind in his First Piano Concerto, in C major, Opus 15; and back of this lies the popular Mozart concerto in the same key, No. 21, K. 467. With Mozart, revealingly, this forceful canonic statement at the end of the ritornello seems to warn the soloist off: after a show of spirit in a little cadenza, the piano gracefully falls back into a long trill, below which the theme appears once again, quietly, in the orchestra. In the ritornello of Beethoven's Third, the arrival of the theme in its new angry guise feels like a challenge to the soloist. For Beethoven does another unusual thing: he writes a very heavy stop with a fermata at the point of cadence. High noon! One can almost see solo and orchestra glaring at each other across this aporia.

Elemental and electric, three upward scales in octaves sweep up from the depths to the heights in a way that no orchestral instrument can do [3:21]. This was inspired, if the idea was to show the soloist in the best possible light. The scales deflect attention from volume to range, from weight to mobility, giving the reciprocal playing of the first theme new vital energy. Lifted by the scales, the theme is played very high, higher than Mozart ever wrote for a piano: the solo reaches up to high G, a note that had been added to the piano compass shortly before the C-minor Concerto was premiered. This solo instrument carves out its own space—literally.

Acting as a sort of fractured *Eingang,* this gesture whips up excitement for the theme that is coming, like a minuscule version of Chaikovsky's ploy in his Violin Concerto. The scales are improvisatory in spirit, if not improvised. Sketched as early as 1796, completed in 1803,[5] Concerto No. 3 has one pedal, as it were, in the Romantic nineteenth century and one pedal in the Classical eighteenth.

The listener is never allowed to forget this striking solo entrance. Beethoven brings it back at later junctures, later aporias: for example, after the second ritornello prior to the development section. This ritornello ends more tamely than the first (no canonic exclamations, no fermata), and while the piano's upward scales still sound explosive, they no longer explore the unknown. Instead they look within and interrogate the theme. For the first time the drumbeat ending of the theme is analyzed out, and at once the new fragment is taken over in the woodwinds and strings in imitation and in considerable hushed excitement. The three-beat drum rhythm ⁻ ᵕ ⁻ ᵕ ⁻ continues to be heard, as an incitement and background to solo developments that are new and newly eloquent [7:36]. A derivative of the drum rhythm persists up to the point of recapitulation.

Here Beethoven brings the first theme in its most forceful version yet, as he was always inclined to do. The first phrase is fortissimo, and the second no longer piano but fortissimo also, blared out by the wind band. Out of the blue come quiet iterations of the drum figure in the same harmonic configuration as at the start of the development section—now interspersed with expressive arpeggios from the piano. The concerto agents suddenly find themselves engaged in intimate conversation [9:34].

Engaged: nothing has prepared us for the muted drama of this passage. Its rhetorical force is harder to specify than what it accomplishes. It deflates the fortissimo or, rather, it defuses the fortissimo by deflecting attention to something understated—understated but arresting because of the freight it is carrying from earlier in the work. Not all of those sometimes brutal recapitulations in early Beethoven are handled as diplomatically as this.

Right after the cadenza, in a famous uncanny passage, the three-beat drum figure is heard again. If the concerto's first theme could be said to have undergone a motivic analysis at the beginning of the development section, in the coda it undergoes a sonic analysis, for here the three-beat drum figure is actually played by the drums—at long last. Consciously or not, we have been awaiting this inevitable sound [15:01].[6] The drums come forward in the final ritornello, a place where tradition would have the solo quit and leave it to the band to wrap up all proceedings. (It does not quit; Beethoven was listening to Mozart's Piano Concerto in C minor, not to tradition.) And once again—this is the third time—the drum figure inspires the solo to a new fertile invention, an unexpected moment of pathos prior to the final march to the cadence.

Meanwhile, it has not escaped notice that in the later part of the movement the drum figure has been working alone, without the scales. (They are not present after the second time, though they are kept in mind by multioctave downward scales at the ends of the piano's bravura sections.) Beethoven restores the balance at the last moment. In the last three bars, upward octave scales, and more of them than ever, *stringendo*, sweep up past the extraterrestrial high G all the way up to high C, three octaves above middle C [15:42]. The composer was trading in fortepiano futures here: although a few instruments with an extended range up to high C did apparently exist as early as 1800, Beethoven's many piano compositions up to that time never made use of one. When he stormed the heights with those scales at the premiere, how electrifying they must have sounded on his brand-new Erard instrument! They get lost, paradoxically, on the mighty Steinway.

⌐ In the piano's beginning, then, is its end. In between beginning and end, the solo has touched on and defined and linked in memory the concerto's most interesting, inventive, and eloquent moments so far. The solo's entrance music and its continuation become a fluid vinculum holding together a structure that is in fact otherwise stiff and minimally expressive. In short, then, and in summary: what I am saying is that in the Beethoven Third Concerto, it's getting started that makes the music go.

Particularity and Polarity 2

At a conference a good many years ago, I read a paper on Beethoven's codas, provoked in part by what I maintained was the unaccountable neglect by *Formenlehre* theorists of the coda as a component of sonata form. The paper was illustrated with many short recorded excerpts taken from just the ends of Beethoven compositions. After the presentation, an old friend came up as people do to offer his congratulations. That, he said, was the most hilarious paper he had ever heard. He probably would have found the first of these Norton Lectures, "Getting Started," with its long string of aborted snippets from the *beginnings* of concertos, every bit as comical.

However, by the end of that lecture I did come around to discuss, if not an entire piece, at least an entire movement, by—who else?—Beethoven, from his Third Piano Concerto. I even played a coda.

Now as it happens neither Beethoven nor the coda occurs by whim in my work as a critic. I come from a tradition that privileges accounts of musical compositions taken as wholes—complete operas, complete string quartets, complete concertos—over other critical projects. The concept of the entire can shade easily into the completed, the fulfilled, the absolute, even the perfect, all under the aegis of what might be called the coda syndrome. And my generation is now reproached, with some justice, for its adherence to the idea of the authority of the work of art, sometimes erroneously equated with the autonomy of the work of art. Termination, "the sense of an ending," in Frank Kermode's phrase—a more usual term for musicians is closure—has been among our preoccupations. Beethoven, the great terminator, has been our hero. "We are in love with the idea of fulfillment," Kermode has written, "and our interpretations show it."[1]

Sensitive to these reproaches, I thought of getting started in the present project by addressing openings and especially solo entries: moments of juncture and breach, aporias, second only to the complete breakdown represented by the cadenza, the concerto's notorious moment of carnival. Later there will be more to say about cadenzas, too.

Meanwhile, since old habits and old convictions die hard, at the end of the present lecture you will hear about more than one entire concerto, three movements taken together as a whole. In fact, this second lecture will be altogether more sweeping than the first. For it begins, somewhat gingerly, with first principles. What is a concerto?

・ン・ン・ン

For answers to questions like that one turns, needless to say, to the *Harvard Dictionary of Music*. To quote from the concise edition: "concerto: Since the late 18th century, a composition for orchestra and a solo instrument, though in the 17th and 18th centuries also a composition for orchestra and a small group of solo instruments."[2] While one could perhaps quibble about those ballpark dates, one must applaud the *Harvard Dictionary's* immediate recourse to the historical. A banal fact: the concerto has changed over its three-hundred-year history. Otherwise it would not have survived to postdate, as well as predate, the symphony. The pioneer of the solo concerto, Giuseppe Torelli, published his first works in 1692 and 1698, and the greatly admired concerti grossi of Corelli are thought to have been composed earlier, though not published till later. Concertos are still being composed at a good rate today, often commissioned by important performers and underwritten by foundations, and they often get their first performances as part of the package. Mstislav Rostropovich has stimulated an entire repertory: pieces by Prokofiev, Shostakovich, Britten, Bliss, Piston, Bernstein, Penderecki, Lutosławski, Arvo Pärt, Bernard Rands, and dozens of other composers.

Concise *Harvard* continues: "An essential feature of [the genre] is the contrast between passages dominated by the soloist (usually requiring some display of virtuosity) and passages (called *tutti*) for the orchestra alone." Now more substantial quibbles arise. "Essential": critics today are more wary of essences than they were when the *Harvard Dictionary* was first compiled. No doubt contrast is intrinsic to the concerto. To declare it essential, however, is to make a seemingly small move that privileges it decisively and even coercively over, let us say, virtuosity. Notice that the dictionary has the phrase "usually requiring some display of virtuosity" in parentheses. Virtuosity is literally marginalized.

Is contrast really "essential" to the concerto, more than virtuosity? The musical criticism of modernism inclined toward abstraction and dialectic; it had little to say about the physicalities of music. When Thomas Clifton, in his profound book *Music as Heard,* remarked briskly: "Reconciliation, as an essence, is constitutive of every concerto I have ever heard,"[3] he was evoking a familiar model of the art work as a nexus of disparate elements awaiting unification or closure. Not all concertos accommodate to this model. The concerto entails duality, but duality does not always mean contrast, let alone conflict destined for reconciliation. My effort will be to lay out and examine the different

Plate 2
Mstislav Rostropovich

modes of duality, the different ways in which concerto duality is expressed or articulated, as the genre has changed over history, and sometimes changed back again.

Before beginning, we need a general term to use for the two things that contrast or do not contrast in a concerto. To refer to the solo and the orchestra as "sound sources" seems bland and for some reason also unidiomatic; better is the German term *Klangkörper,* "sound-bodies," because that keeps in mind the physicality of the concerto. And how often concerto sound-bodies are spoken of as though they were actual bodies! And how significant. People habitually personify them as human agents, and "agent" will be my term of preference.

Already in the eighteenth century concerto agents were likened to the protagonist and the chorus in Greek drama. The music theorist Heinrich Christoph Koch enlarged on the analogy with some enthusiasm:

> One finds a passionate conversation between the solo and the accompanying orchestra, to whom the former confides his feelings, while the latter with its short, interspersed phrases now signals its approval, as though to affirm his sentiment; now seeks to rally his exalted emotion even further, in the Allegro; now commiserates with him or consoles him, in the Adagio. For me, in short, the concerto represents at times something rather like the tragedy of the ancients, where the actor lays open his feelings not to the parterre but to the chorus. As for the chorus, it is intimately bound up with the action, while at the same time it is empowered to take part in the expression of sentiment.[4]

In the nineteenth century the agents were generally seen as antagonists in an unequal struggle, between "the powerful, inexhaustibly richly colored orchestra" and its "small, insignificant, but strong-minded adversary," as Chaikovsky put it in a well-known letter to Mme. von Meck. Stravinsky, working at some sort of piano concerto (it was never finished) in 1911, envisaged a puppet "exasperating the patience of the orchestra with diabolical cascades of arpeggi";[5] as is well known, this project turned into the mimetic ballet *Petrushka,* in the score of which a prominent piano part testifies to the music's origin. For Elgar, Nielsen, and Berg, the violin in their violin concertos represented a woman for whom they had special feelings (women, in Berg's case). In Hans Werner Henze's Second Violin Concerto, the soloist mugs and speaks, wears a costume, and switches violins.

What is the intrinsic character, the particularity of each sound-body, or agent? If one starts with Chaikovsky's "powerful and richly colored" versus "small, insignificant, but strong-minded," the next step is to recognize that during much of the concerto's history, the sound-bodies have also differed in their participation in certain basic musical activities. As agents, they assume functions keyed to their characters. I once called these functions *discourse* and *display,* favoring the linguistic term "discourse" over the mathematical term "logic" to refer in the broadest terms to the ongoing play of musical material and rhetoric, musical process, music's illusion of movement and import.[6] Theme, tonality, rhythm, texture, dynamics: these are some of the carriers of traditional musical discourse. Musical discourse takes place quintessentially in the symphony, the orchestral genre par excellence. The discipline that deals with musical discourse is musical analysis.

Display, on the other hand, is a primal quality of music-making that can exist at low levels of discourse. Display is playing loud and fast and singing sexy; display can be extemporaneous, unpredictable, out of control, refractory to musical analysis. An orchestra cannot do and be these things—its music has to be composed, like a composed salad. If there are genres of Western music in which solo display is repressed, the concerto is not among them. A concerto without virtuosity would not be worth the name; it would probably be called a symphony with a solo part, in fact. Of course the solo instrument also participates in the concerto's discourse, sharing this with the orchestra, and sometimes taking the lion's share. Yet it can also pursue virtuosity at the expense of, even in the absence of, discourse.

᠁ ᠁ ᠁

All this is encapsulated in the opening bars of Beethoven's "Emperor" Concerto, Piano Concerto No. 5 in E-flat, Opus 73, of 1809. Beethoven Track 2 has this knack of projecting basic gestural qualities of music, below or almost below the level of discourse; this quality, I am sure, is what astounded Beethoven's contemporaries and also what still earns this composer his disproportionate pie-slice of the musical canon, to the disquiet of some observers. I am not the first to identify this music as a concerto archetype. Beethoven presents themeless, rhythmless essences here—the essence of weight and the essence of virtuoso display. Single full-orchestra chords, fortissimo. Cascades of piano arabesque between them. The display sounds improvisatory, and is meant to sound impro-visatory, even though every note was written out by the composer. Weight translates as power, for the orchestra's four mighty chords—the tonic triad, subdominant, dominant, and tonic again—map out the lowest common denominator of musical form, the harmonic structure underpinning every Classical composition. The chords are not only weighty, they are on the deepest level functional. Writ large, this primi-tive discourse holds the power to organize and articulate musical form.

"The essence of weight" and "the essence of virtuosity"—no, the word "essence" is (again) not right, for as I shall try to show, the functional, operative characteristics of the solo and orchestra agents change under different circumstances. It makes no sense to talk about essences that keep changing. The term *particularity*, meaning no more than the distinctive characteristics of the solo and the orchestra in any particular context, lacks the implication of immanence conveyed by "essence," and though it may generate some peculiar locutions, it seems best for our purposes. In some situations the particularity of the orchestral agent can be said to be weight, in others discourse, in others the primal, and so on; and likewise with the solo agent. Over the course of the concerto's history, new particularities have been constructed in different periods by different composers.

How striking it is that Beethoven's magnificent demonstration of concerto particularities should refer, in fact, to the concerto of the Baroque era. Beethoven in 1809 was celebrating an archaic ideal. While the "Emperor" is routinely cited as the prototype for the confrontational thrust of the nineteenth-century concerto, this introductory passage tells only of a potential for confrontation. The agents do not engage with each other; the boxers touch gloves ahead of time, they don't fight. I have already used the word "polarity" for this mode of duality. The agents are here, at least for the moment, polarized.

The master of Baroque polarity was of course Vivaldi. Vivaldi published his most celebrated concertos under the title *Il cimento dell' armonia e l'inventione,* usually translated as the contest between harmony and invention; actually *cimento* means a hazardous trial or ordeal, so one could also say the trial of organization and spontaneity, or as I should like to put it, the crux of discourse and display. This polarity determines Baroque concerto form. Beethoven's functional chords in the "Emperor" Concerto introduction are tonic, subdominant, dominant, tonic—I IV V I—and it is not hard to find Baroque pieces in which this same generic foundation-work is composed out, as the music theorists say, on the higher level of musical form. To cite one instance, in a C-minor violin concerto from Vivaldi's *La Cetra,* Opus 9 No. 11, the ritornello launches the first movement in the tonic key as a 16-bar closed paragraph; then, interspersed with relatively long episodes of solo display, the ritornello returns successively and weightily in whole or in part in several other keys (mediant, subdominant, and dominant); and then it returns for the last time in the tonic, anchoring the music down. Beethoven's harmonic foundation-work is I IV V I, Vivaldi's is I III iv v I.

The markers of the form are set apart and emphasized in the Baroque concerto more than in other contemporary genres of instrumental music. Polarity extends from the initial juxtaposition of first ritornello and first solo section to define the form of a whole.

• ༞ • ༞ • ༞

The idea of polarity is what Bach found interesting in Vivaldi: that, not Vivaldi's particularities. Bach became fascinated by polarity as a principle of musical form *tout court,* in genres such as the sonata, the cantata, the fugue, and so on as well as in concertos. The influence of Vivaldi on his northern admirer has been analyzed at length by musicologists, and exhibit A on the dissection table is always the collection of about two dozen Italian concertos that Bach transcribed for keyboard instruments, early in his career. Most of these concertos are polarized: the orchestra plays one thing, the solo plays something else. Bach certainly understood his models, and in the great demonstration piece that he wrote much later, and advertised as *ein Concerto nach Italienischen Gusto,* the Italian Concerto for Harpsichord from the *Clavier-Übung,* ritornello and solo material are entirely independent.

Yet Bach's own true concertos move decisively in the direction of reciprocity: the solo either adopts or responds to musical material from the ritornello. Orchestra and solo share music between them. When this happens in Vivaldi, in about a third of the works, the solo does little more than tip its hat to the first motif of the ritornello, before it settles in to virtuoso display.[7] With Bach the figures are just the reverse. Less than five percent of his concerto movements are polarized, and the salutations are nearly always much more effusive. In Bach an entire ritornello may be retraced by solo arabesque and other action.

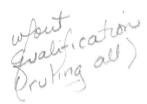

w/out qualification (ruling all)

It is a little curious that two of Bach's best loved concertos should be among the few that are polarized. Both are in D minor, which seems hardly enough to account for another curious thing, the similarities between them: in both first and last movements, the openings of the ritornellos sound rather similar, as though one concerto were viewing the other through a more sophisticated lens (the solos sound quite different). Also, both first-movement ritornellos feature distinctive, unusual musical textures. The earlier of these two works, transcribed by Bach from an original concerto for violin, is the Concerto in D minor for Harpsichord, where the ritornello is in unison and octaves throughout. The other is the Concerto in D minor for Two Violins. Here the texture is fugue; this is Bach's only concerto to start out with a full-fledged fugal ritornello. In a slightly irregular exposition—irregular in Bach's always logical way—four fugal voices enter at 4-bar (and one 5-bar) intervals, moving from I to v to I to v to iv; then a final tonic entry brings the ritornello to a punctual tonic close. The original ritornello is 21 bars long. All the subsequent ritornellos last for 4 bars, the length of the fugue subject.

Bach was, it seems, reconsidering the question of orchestral particularity here. Fugue in his time provided the preeminent vehicle for the discursive, and he makes this ritornello not only majestic and weighty, as per the specifications of his contemporary J. J. Quantz, but also complex and intellectual. Perhaps the reason for the polarization of Bach's Two-Violin Concerto is that at this stage he didn't want to allow his new fugal agent to be confused with the solo agent. A more richly developed example of the same syndrome can be found in an organ work in concerto form—polarized concerto form: the "Wedge" Fugue in E minor.

It may seem strange to bring up a much later composer in this connection: Chaikovsky. Yet Chaikovsky had an analogous idea for orchestral particularity. To be sure, what counted as intellectual content for him was not fugue, but motivic development in the German, Beethovenian *Gusto*. For development the concerto orchestra must look to the symphony, where this principle reaches its apogee. There will be more to say about this in the next lecture.

In any case, the Two-Violin Concerto is the exception that proves the rule; in Bach's concertos the rule is reciprocity. And reciprocity was also the wave of the future. Although the thirty-odd concertos of Sebastian Bach scarcely circulated outside of Leipzig and his own circle (and Brandenburg, presumably), his impact on the genre has been traced through his cosmopolitan and influential sons Carl Philipp Emanuel and Johann Christian. Mozart as a child met J. C. Bach in London and expressed his affection for the man and his music in various ways, including the composition of some early piano concertos derived from the older composer's work, and quotations from his work in later concertos.[8] For the junior Bachs, for Mozart and Beethoven, for the Classical era and beyond, reciprocity was the principle applied not only to the solo entry, but in concept at least to every element of the composition.

This too is matter for the next lecture. For now, we skip ahead for some polarities in later transformations.

Not surprisingly, polarities made a comeback in the Neoclassical era, the era of Hindemith and Stravinsky. In fact the concerto can probably claim status as the Neoclassical genre *par excellence*. Both modernist masters contributed to it generously, under the name "concerto" or under other names, and the telltale fragrance of the Bach concertos can be sniffed in much other music of the time (*eau de Brandenbourg*, we might call it). A prime example is Stravinsky's first concerto, the Concerto for Piano and Wind Instruments of 1924.

In this work, a special target for Stravinsky's detractors and no special favorite, it seems, of his admirers, the polarity is an original one, a construction of the composer. The particularity of the solo agent is a new kind of piano sound: dry, staccato, with no pedal; and if thick chords are used they are used only for percussive effects and hence cut short. No doubt the twang of Wanda Landowska's harpsichord, first bruited in 1903, contributed to the mix; certainly the spare style of the Bach Inventions did, perhaps also some initiatives by Prokofiev. An early archetype that everyone knows, from 1911, is the player-piano sound of the Russian Dance in *Petrushka*. This music, as I have already mentioned, started life as a *Konzertstück*. There was a real meeting of minds when Stravinsky had to work up his technique in order to play his concerto and other works in public and turned happily to Czerny ("the greatest composer for the piano").[9]

The orchestral agent in the Concerto for Piano and Winds is also original: a wind band—double reeds, four horns, trumpets, and trombones[10]—in various segments but always very closely knit and always fixated on the same very simple material, a sort of dirge. Just as the new brittle piano style mocks late Romantic pianism, this dirge mocks the lush orchestral sounds in the late Romantic concerto of Anton Rubinstein, Chaikovsky, and Rachmaninoff. If Stravinsky's piano style builds on the Russian Dance in *Petrushka,* his orchestra looks back to the chorales in *L'Histoire du soldat* and the Symphonies of Wind Instruments.

These novel agencies form a polarity, and this polarity is first displayed quite in Vivaldi's manner, if the comparison may be permitted with material that is so unlike Vivaldi, and with agents that ambulate at such different rates: the first being a Largo, the second Allegro. As in some Vivaldi concertos, too, the solo at its entrance makes a light reciprocal reference to the opening motif of the ritornello, which is *do te do,* played in the rhythm of Chopin's Funeral March, more or less. The piano tweaks this into something almost jazzy. If this means to pay homage to Vivaldi, it also means to parody. Stravinsky tips his hat to Vivaldi, and gives him the finger at the same time.

Thus begins a dizzy parade of frivolous material proposed by the piano with much assistance from the orchestra, playing now in a much more open, more chamber-musical way. Frivolity is, exactly, a component of the solo particularity, a counter-dirge. If prewar *Petrushka* evokes the music of a Russian carnival, Stravinsky's postwar music sends up the music of Parisian nightlife, Bach in the bordello, "Bach with smallpox," according to an irritated compatriot, Prokofiev. The piano's rat-a-tat pulse seldom misses a beat or a fraction of a beat: that counts as an important component of its particularity. The ideal, the composer declared, was mechanical regularity.

After a time the flux settles into a sort of stiff piano cadenza, and as this resolves into a climactic appearance of the dirge, the polarity surfaces again. A great tutti emerges for the first time; an earlier generation would have called it sublime—exhilarating and terrifying in its sheer plenitude and intricacy, both rhythmic and textural. The solo and its pulse can still be heard, merged or fused into a unique composite texture presided over by the orchestra. Originally the solo parodied the dirge and brushed it aside. Now the solo is both superimposed upon the orchestra and encased by it.

·‐ The slow movement of the Concerto for Piano and Winds is the serious, heavy statement placed in between two very light ones. It demands our attention even though, like Vivaldi's slow movements, it knows nothing of the polarity of the other movements, or perhaps exactly because of that know-nothingness. More traditional in style and intent, this movement is all about singing, like most slow movements—

Example 8

Example 9

or at least, it's about trying to sing. For there is a problem. How can the new piano agent, devised for percussion and pulse and parody—how can this new piano sing?

Yet the opening piano melody unquestionably aspires to expressive lyricism, in spite of unlikely attributes such as prevailing downward motion, cramped range, and ponderous left-hand chords. Expressive detail comes from a simple turn-motif *mi fa sol |fa—mi* and its derivative *mi fa sol |la——*. This supplies a mild climax. The heart of the movement, framed by two passionate piano outbursts marked "Cadenza, *poco rubato*" (which rubato, incidentally, shatters Stravinsky's "ideal of mechanical regularity"), has various solo instruments playing simple phrases in the Chaikovskian vein that Stravinsky so often tapped for lyricism. The quiet piano accompaniment to these phrases recalls Satie, perhaps. The piano seems to be covertly watching the oboe and the flute and the French horn, as though from behind a screen, enviously.

Example 10

At the end of the movement the first melody returns, in an admirably drafted free version. Piano and orchestra begin together, in a high register, but as the piano soon drops out, the melody in its new manifestation belongs to the winds. The piano rejoins them only when they hit bottom—a thoroughly downbeat place for the piano to recall the climax of the original tune, *mi fa sol |la——*. My sense here is not of the piano's success in supplying certain functional elements to the melody, but rather of its newly exposed failure to sing the melody all the way through, as it had done at the start, however clumpily. The piano reiterates its *la* in a hesitant, moving way. Something in the intermediate lyrical discourse has depressed the solo voice.

Example 11

·⤳ Polarity returns in the finale. The solo leads off with a stream of lively trivia, once again, more pointed than ever in its persiflage. There

Track 3

is a cakewalk, a couple of tawdry marches, and a parody of a certain *Well-Tempered Clavier* fugue. The metronome mark is identical to that of the first movement, with an only slightly less machine-like pulse laid down by the piano.

It is all the more arresting, then, when after some time the chatter suddenly stops and the piano is left gasping slowly on a single chord, many times repeated [3:23]. Paralysis! The new tempo is enough to recall the Largo of the dirge, and this indeed begins to regroup itself with characteristic wind sounds and rhythms. The winds, sounding glum, also recall that mildly climactic fragment of the slow-movement melody, *mi fa sol |la——*; and with a single marvelous soft rolled chord the piano acknowledges and accepts its own former incapacity [3:44]. During the playing of the dirge that ensues (to be exact, three-fifths of the original dirge), all the piano can utter is the opening motif *do te do:* a frail and I think pathetic recall of its original parody. The greater part of the dirge is played by the orchestra alone [3:49]. It is all very bleak.

Bang! The brittle piano chatter returns for a jokey codetta. A very short ending: about ten seconds [4:25].

It turns out, then, that the studied Baroque appropriation at the beginning of the piece, where the agents are polarized *à la* Vivaldi, is no more than an opening gambit. Later on Stravinsky treats his newly constructed agents in a manner that owes nothing to Vivaldi or Bach. At the end of the first movement, one agent is engulfed, astonishingly, by the other. At the end of the finale, their interplay becomes almost palpably narrative—an attribute despised by the Neoclassicists, of course, as the detritus of Romanticism.

It is not hard to make out the story (or make up the story) if one thinks back to the *Konzertstück* that turned into *Petrushka* and the well-known account Stravinsky gave of its genesis. "I had in mind," he says in his autobiography, a distinct picture of a puppet, suddenly endowed with life, exasperating the patience of the orchestra with diabolical cascades of *arpeggi;* the latter in turn retaliates with menacing trumpet-blasts. There follows a terrible brawl which on reaching its climax ends up with the sorrowful and plaintive collapse of the poor puppet.[11]

The tendency to personify concerto agents seems irresistible, for Neoclassicist and Romantic alike. Piano and orchestra are already half humanized in Stravinsky's puppet fantasy, and the ballet itself completes this process. Petrushka in the Russian Dance of Act I, scene 1 is pure puppet, and he is a puppet in the final scene, too, when after the frightened passers-by have seen him cut down by the scimitar of the Blackamoor, the Mountebank shows them, merely, a bag of sticks and stuffing. In the center and heart of the ballet, however, the puppet acquires attributes of personhood. He learns to feel desire, jealousy, and vulnerability. At the final curtain, from above the puppet theater an inspirited Petrushka returns, crying like a real boy, proclaiming his humanity.

The bi-faceted piano of the Concerto for Piano and Winds much of the time behaves like a dancing puppet. Disciplined at the end of the first movement, this exasperating character turns up again in the last movement full of fight. But in the slow movement the piano has tried to sing and even (in the cadenzas) to speak. Octatonic flourishes introduce the two cadenzas, recalling those splendid octatonic fanfares which cry out in the ballet as the emblem of Petrushka's humanity. In the concerto, just as in the ballet, humanization entails human pathos. Near the end of the third movement the piano's failure in the second is recalled and compounded. Like Petrushka, the inspirited piano is cut down.

The action is less graphic than in the ballet, naturally, and it reaches a different, almost an opposite outcome. In the very short codetta of the concerto finale, it is the dancing puppet that returns: Petrushka proclaiming his subhumanity.[12]

That is one possible take on Stravinsky's provocative Concerto for Piano and Winds. I shall have more to say about it later.

.ᵔ .ᵔ .ᵔ

For Béla Bartók in the 1920s, Stravinsky was a commanding presence, an inspiration, and a major problem. Bartók worked out (or at) this problem in both his First Piano Concerto of 1926 and his Second of 1931. The latter presents his extensive thoughts on concerto particularity and concerto polarity.

The slow movement comes to mind first, surely: the extraordinary Adagio. It is scored initially for string instruments alone, with mutes. They whisper a chorale, using a weird diatonic dissonant harmonic style made for this occasion and never used anywhere else, so far as I know, and also exploiting an array of string special effects. Then the piano comes in, working its way up to a desperate lamentation locked into pedal-timpani trills. Bartók has invented two unique, rather amazing, and utterly polarized agents here; they make no contact.

While neither particularity is exactly a ray of sunshine in itself, what makes this the true music of despair is the polarity, the mutual incomprehension. Only in the very last bars does polarity lapse or yield, the low strings inching up and actually meeting the piano as it sinks down into a consonant dyad. The final cadence that sounds both improbable and inevitable—that is a well-known Bartók trademark. In the present case cadential reciprocity, relation, and reconciliation seem to issue through clenched teeth.

On another level, another polarity informs this movement. The Adagio appears at the beginning and end of the movement with an entirely different Presto occurring in between. For the most part, this central music cannot be identified as solo nor in the ordinary sense orchestral. Rather it is a blend of the two, a diffused texture in which the piano behaves as though it were a member of an expanded orchestra. The gross disparity between the Presto and the Adagio can therefore be regarded as also a polarity, if not between concerto agents, then between concerto textures.

Still another, altogether different polarity controls the outer movements of the Second Piano Concerto. Getting started in this work is not a discreet cough, not a sigh, not a rustle, not a starting gun, but an alarm bell. The piano's alarum is answered by a trumpet fanfare, after which the piano practically quotes from the Russian Dance in *Petrushka*. The brass and the piano motifs are so similar that the listener is prepared to accept them as antecedent and consequent, as a single composite idea. But that, we discover, is not how they work, and disentangling them becomes the first item of business—business that almost stops the music dead in its tracks. The brass motif is isolated and prolonged by canons, and henceforth serves as a ritornello very much in Vivaldi's spirit (bars 25–31).

Just as Stravinsky's percussive piano regressed to the fundament of piano sound-production, namely hammering, so Bartók's orchestra—an orchestra without strings, in the first movement—regresses to primal brass-instrument behavior, namely the sounding forth of fanfares. An early definition of a fanfare, cited in *Grove's Dictionary*, "a mixture of arpeggios and runs," describes exactly what Bartók has. Fanfares are eminently ad hoc, "unreflective improvisations" designed for maximum noise, a hundred trumpets and fifes on a good day, one on the heels of the other. So Bartók's fanfares are never the same; the fanfare motif can be treated to inversion and retrograde, with the runs coming before the arpeggios. It always makes a sumptuous noise.

The relation of this new orchestral agent to the rest of the music— music that is dominated by the piano as completely as in Stravinsky— is, once again, polar. The fanfare and the *Petrushka* theme are similar, and so there are occasional moments of flirtation between them, includ-

Example 12

ing one that is rather coy: but no engagement. After the beginning, with its moment of ambiguity, the fanfare neither answers nor comments; it simply punctuates. The piano finally gets a real hold of the fanfare motif only in the cadenza, an ambivalent element in concerto form that stands both within the official discourse and outside it.

Now, in the concerto's third movement all the material from the first movement comes back transformed, in a different tempo, meter, and so on (a favorite procedure with this composer; he also follows it in his Violin Concerto). The ritornello-like fanfares and all the solo flights return—but this is only the kernel of Bartók's idea. The third movement is also to be a rondo. This form is the traditional—in fact tired—ending ploy for concertos, one that no twentieth-century composer could use innocently. By its nature a rondo has a main theme as its *raison d'être* and is ruled by that main theme, so the blocks of first-movement material that return transformed in Bartók's finale start out feeling like traditional rondo episodes in between commanding statements of the main theme. They feel subsidiary, in spite of all the freight they are carrying from earlier times, the more so on account of the vitality of the rondo theme itself, a sort of superior *Allegro barbaro*.

Track 4

But it is the fanfare that perseveres and stays the course when the rondo theme, after four splendid utterances, fades. A simple thing: the fanfare takes over from the rondo theme as the organizing principle for this finale [1:02, 2:10, 3:22, 5:21]. Just as in the first movement, fanfares blare away at the end, unfazed by a new *Petrushka* quotation. A single polarity emerges as the organizing principle for the entire concerto.

The terms of this polarity remain to be clarified; let me try to do so. The particularity of the piano agent in this piece is not to be identified with the Stravinsky piano sound, Bach with pockmarks—this in spite of Bartók's almost defiant *Petrushka* references, near-quotations from the

Bach Two-Part Inventions, and mechanical regularity aplenty. For the piano does so many other things in addition to this: it whirls, waltzes, stomps, shimmers . . . It is, in fact, unusually various and unusually inventive. With the rondo theme, too, the piano's variations each time are dazzling and radical, quite out of the ordinary [1:15, 2:26, 3:52].

I hear the solo particularity here as spontaneity. "Exuberance" is the word for it in an old essay by Mosco Carner.[13] Improvisation, one of the piano's basic faculties—a basic faculty of any musical instrument— shines brightest, or can be made to shine brightest, when a solo instrument plays together with a group. Spontaneity is by no means confined to cadenzas. And this faculty is deployed extensively in the Second Piano Concerto, more so than in other works by Bartók, as Mosco Carner noted: extensively and, I think, programmatically.

The juxtaposition of brass-band basics and piano spontaneity, then, produces the overarching polarity in Bartók's concerto (meaning the polarity that arches over the slow movement. The slow movement presents its own nest of further polarities). And very strikingly, what Bartók has contrived here is something like the reverse of the ancient orchestra/solo, discourse/display polarity. It is the orchestra that flaunts the sub-discursive or the primal, with its signals from the hunt and the battlefield, varied but essentially undeveloped. The solo delivers and develops a whole array of sophisticated musical delights.

•‿ So much for the essentialism of concerto essences. As for the remarkable spontaneous quality of this concerto, a precedent for it can be found in an obvious enough place, in the work of a composer who was important to Bartók before he ever heard a note of Stravinsky. Liszt has already figured peripherally in our discussion, and he will make a more emphatic showing later on, when we return to improvisation and its basic role in virtuoso music-making.

Reciprocity, Roles, and Relationships

3

First impressions can be very important for a concerto soloist, a fact that Beethoven hammers home in his Piano Concerto No. 3, as we have seen. Vivaldi liked to have the solo enter after the opening ritornello with polarized material of a virtuosic character. Mozart, less splashy, preferred to have the solo hark back to the opening music of the ritornello reciprocally, remembering it, proposing a relation.

Polarity and reciprocity: one can usefully extend the range of these two concepts. I have already proposed that polarity can be seen as the organizing principle of Baroque concerto form in the early eighteenth century. On reflection, this is perhaps a rather obvious idea. It may hold more interest as applied to certain concertos of the twentieth century. In any case, one item to be explored here is the analogous proposition that reciprocity became the main organizing principle for the concerto in the late eighteenth and nineteenth centuries. And to develop this thought, it will be necessary to speak in broader terms than I have been doing up to now.

Reciprocity, as I want to use the concept, covers more than just openings and solo entries, more than the interchange between the agents at this or that specific point, and the resulting local interplay. It covers all aspects of the musical discourse, a global field of mutual awareness within which concerto action can develop. The concerto agents hear each other and respond accordingly. Thus reciprocity becomes the enabling condition for concerto dialogue—the conversation of these lectures' *double entendre* title.

"Conversation" was also Goethe's word, in a well-known remark he made not about the concerto but about the string quartet.[1] Obviously dialogue is not unique to the concerto as a genre. Here, though, voices are raised as they must not be—cannot be—in a quartet; the dissimilar agents address each other in livelier tones, easier to overhear and perhaps easier to analyze. Concerto conversation can sometimes resemble a public shouting match, though at other times it does not lack for the intimacy cherished by Goethe. With the eighteenth-century concerto, in any case, the distinction between orchestral and chamber music should not be exaggerated. Bach's Third Brandenburg Concerto is properly performed as a nonet with continuo, and much later concertos were on occasion played as chamber music—as late as the Beethoven Fourth Piano Concerto and the concertos of Chopin.[2] Mozart was only able to publish concertos when he was prepared to provide optional wind parts allowing for performances of this kind.

The works of Mozart, Beethoven, Schumann, Liszt, Brahms, and Chaikovsky provide us with luminous models of concerto dialogue: a formidable body of music, widely loved and admired. Because of these strong feelings, however, there is an inclination to take conversation and all that goes with it as an essence. It can become a defining feature of the genre, a sine qua non for the interest and value of individual concertos. Musicians and critics are alert today, more than we were, to the marginalization of various musical repertories, and I believe that this is a case in point: for some listeners and critics, concertos predicated on reciprocity block out the very sight and sound of other concertos. For some, indeed, the Mozart corpus alone is quite sufficient to effect this blockage. That this marginalization has been institutional as well as personal goes without saying.

One message that should come through in these concerto conversations is that there are other modes of concerto duality (starting with polarity, of course); composers have availed themselves of other resources besides reciprocity. After Brahms, no doubt its greatest master, composers have tended to back away from reciprocity—sometimes all the way back. This is something to bear in mind as we now begin a fairly extended conversation on reciprocity and its ramifications.

＊＊＊

Reciprocity extends beyond concerto openings and solo entries. Reciprocity also embraces more than the interchange of similar material between the concerto agents; more is involved than one agent "repeating" the music of the other. Scare quotes spring up around the word "repeating," because concerto repetitions are very different from repetitions marked with vertical lines and dots in marches for band or sonatinas for piano. Consider Schumann's Piano Concerto. It begins (after a piano flourish) with almost the same melody played first by a woodwind group and then by the solo piano. Yet the difference between the two voices registers at once: in the warm, tactile piano chords after the heterogeneous texture of the wind band, in the telltale initial grace note—and in the dynamic: for the dynamic mark *p* applied to piano chords makes for a gentler sound than *p* applied to a group of seven wind instruments, where it merely mutes their natural stridency. If this counts as an instance of Schumann's notorious weak orchestration, it is weakness with a method. As the music cuts from parade ground to Biedermeier parlor, a public voice is followed by an inward, private one. The theme, we realize, belongs to the piano, not the winds. The piano quietly claims it. Even more quietly, the winds withdraw.

Example 13

Plate 3. Artur Rubinstein and Lorin Maazel

Is this to overinterpret a familiar, seemingly transparent passage of music? Consider it along with the Grieg Piano Concerto, which, if imitation is the sincerest form of flattery, must count as the most prodigal outburst of sincerity in the whole history of the concerto. Neither of the two themes as played by the piano seems to emerge from the sonorous soul of the instrument, as is the case with Schumann. They sound more like passable piano arrangements of the brisk dotted-note figures of the wind band, first, and then of the woodwind and string cantabile. Grieg reminds us, and this was tactless, of the humblest of the roles possible for the piano: its role as a maid of all work who can mimic approximately winds, strings, voices, an orchestra, and so on and so on. Schumann, incidentally, when he found a use later in his first movement for a brisk, martial transformation of his gentle theme, scored it for winds—a casual forecast of the later concerto.

Example 14

The piano may serve as a maid of all work, yet it also commands marvelous sonorities of its own. How well Grieg understood this appears from the crystalline-clamorous piano entry in the second movement of his concerto, after the long orchestral melody. True, this is one more exercise in sincere flattery: Grieg's quarry this time was the "Emperor" Concerto of Beethoven, in his day everyone's favorite all-purpose concerto kit. (Beethoven's piano entry in his slow movement can also be heard echoing in Brahms's Second Piano Concerto, Prokofiev's Fourth, and no doubt others.) Grieg added something fine of his own, a veiled reference to the boisterous piano outburst at the very start of his first movement. That outburst is recollected wistfully, from a new level of awareness encompassing the slow-movement melody.

Example 15

And this I am also calling a reciprocal gesture, even though piano and orchestra have very different music. What matters is the sense of engagement, and the piano here is clearly implicated with the orchestral melody. Its utterance has been prompted by the orchestra, and however unexpected, this utterance is understood as a response to the orchestra. Reciprocity does not always entail echoing or agreeing. It can also encompass contradiction, recoil, retort, reflection, explication, and more.

How is reciprocity in such cases to be distinguished from polarity? I am not able to theorize the distinction, but I am (usually) sure of it on intuitive grounds. If Grieg does not clinch the case, listen to Beethoven's Piano Concerto No. 4 in G major, the Andante con moto movement, a work which has so often been held up as a paradigm of concerto aesthetics. All the way through this much-discussed piece, until just before the end, piano and orchestra have completely different music. Yet generations of listeners have heard these different musics not as independent, but as a precisely modulated series of responses—piano to orchestra, and orchestra to piano. From early times this musical conversation has been read, with a unanimity very rare in Beethoven reception, as a specific narrative: a narrative of harshness and appeal, acquiescence and release, crisis and reconciliation. A narrative of Orpheus, of course, and the Furies.

Reciprocity, then, may involve relations of similitude and relations of dissimilitude, which I distinguish by the terms *replay* and *counterplay*. Counterplay, once again, as in the Grieg slow movement, is not the same as polarity. As for replay, there are of course many kinds that do not involve the exact or nearly the exact same melody, as in the Grieg opening movement and the Schumann. The solo can play a formal variation of the orchestra's theme (and in theory vice versa); Brahms in the second part (the trio) of the second movement of his Second Piano Concerto writes two variations as strict as they are sophisticated. A memorable passage toward the end of Elgar's Cello Concerto has the agents replaying in sequence, that is, using the same motif starting from different pitches, usually lower pitches than the time before. An unusual and beautiful feature of this passage is the solo and orchestra coming together at the end—past the bars shown in Example 16—with

Example 16

the decaying motif in unison and octaves. They coalesce into a single sonority, a new luminous sound, and at the same time each maintains its singularity and its own memory of the dialogue just completed.

Replay can be much more aggressive than that, and in the Romantic era often is. The "Emperor" Concerto, once again, furnished the model followed by, among others, Chaikovsky in his Piano Concerto, where a great confrontation occurs at the same place as in Beethoven's, within the development section of the first movement. Unlike Beethoven, the later composer starts his development with the piano entirely silent, for over a minute. Then it finally breaks in—crashes in—with double-octave scale passages replaying material from the orchestral climax. Chaikovsky doesn't have a Grieg problem; his problem is the transparent setup whereby the Lisztian double octaves have been planted in the orchestra as a foil for the piano's bravura. The increasingly heavy-handed orchestral development is cut off, rejected violently (but so idiomatically) by solo replay; and what happens after this brilliant outburst is a cadenza, the concerto's classic site for virtuosity and improvisation. (In fact the solo in this cadenza invents a new theme, to be taken up briefly by the orchestra.)

Chaikovsky's attitude toward orchestral development I have mentioned before—his regard for it as the intellectual niveau of modern music, the music of Beethoven and the German tradition, manifested archetypically in the symphony. The passage in the Piano Concerto stages a confrontation between particularities: symphonic development versus solo bravura and improvisation. It can be read as a generic critique, a critique of the symphony by the concerto.

The varieties and shades of concerto conversation are limited only by the total sum of the imagination of all concerto composers. I draw attention to just one more type—or is it a cluster?—for which I coin the term *coplay*. A single melody can be shared between, coplayed by, the two agents, so that one completes the thought of the other. Brahms offers two playful examples in the finale of his Second Piano Concerto; in Example 17a, what is replayed is less a melody than a cadential gesture, and in Example 17b a theme returns in coplay that was previously introduced by the orchestra alone. This is a common strategy. Compare the original woodwind statement with a subsequent coplayed version of a theme from Mozart's Piano Concerto No. 23 in E-flat, K. 482. Usually with Mozart, it is the solo that takes over from the orchestra, in a witty or sassy way. Here the orchestra takes over from the piano to enact the last scene in a tragic action, one of only a few represented by this composer: few, but much cherished. Example 17

Example 18

In the main section of the second movement of Schumann's Piano Concerto, the Intermezzo, all or many of these varieties of interplay positively snowball. Scan the entire concerto repertory and you will hardly find a more magical moment. For quartet-like intimacy of conversation it is unique, so far as I know. Example 19

Track 5

•◞ •◞ •◞

Reciprocity can be viewed as a general field of mutual awareness for concerto action, and I should now like to pursue two implications of this concept. The first is its impact on concerto form. The second is its power as the enabling condition for roles and relationships.

Every work of music is its own form, but for the Classical concerto standardized form-templates were in use for the first and the last movements. First-movement form has been studied and expounded at length, by a number of musicologists including some of the most eminent, under the name "Double Exposition Form," "Concerto Sonata Form," or "Ritornello Sonata Form." The form-template for the finale has never been named, so I shall christen it the *mutual rondo*.

•◞ One thing sets mutual rondos apart from rondos in piano sonatas, divertimentos, symphonies, and the like. Every time the rondo theme appears both the solo and the orchestra play it, nearly always in close succession. Typically the solo comes first, with a tune or the beginnings of a tune (sometimes with a pre-existing song or dance tune, as happens a couple of times in Mozart's late piano concertos). That the orchestra typically comes second makes for an agreeable reversal of the order in the opening movements.

Clearly this feature is reciprocal—the orchestra responds to the solo; the orchestra wouldn't play the tune if it hadn't heard the solo—but the reciprocity is not of a very interesting kind. The orchestra does not so much answer the solo theme as confirm it in an enthusiastic spirit. When later the theme comes back two or more times, one listens for this confirmation process almost as much as to the theme itself. As distinct from an ordinary rondo, in a mutual rondo the theme does not just return again and again, it returns accompanied by a BOOSTER to clap it on the back.

What distinguishes this kind of rondo is the readiness with which the thematic replays come—I might go so far as to say the blankness. This much reiteration fixes and formalizes the relationship in a decisive way, whatever else happens in between the repetitions. What happens in between is, needless to say, a good deal. Nonetheless, the pervading sense of mutual rondos from Mozart through Brahms and all the way to the Gershwin Piano Concerto in F is consensus, accommodation, collusion: consensus in aid of play, and in aid of a happy ending.

I have come across one mutual rondo that goes still further, in the finale of a little-known work, Saint-Saëns' Violin Concerto No. 2 in C, Opus 58. There are three conventional enough units presenting the rondo theme in the solo replayed at once by the orchestra. (The last unit is abbreviated, coplayed rather than replayed.) After which, in the coda, Saint-Saëns contrived to extend this ready bonhomie to the movement's second theme, by writing a fugato on this theme, with the solo duly taking its turn with a fugal entry. A small point, and an academic one, in both senses of the word: this piece written in 1858 carries mutuality even a little further than is usually the case in its Classical models.

⸱⤳ The matter of reciprocity and ritornello sonata form (first-movement form) cannot be dealt with so easily. This form-template is a hybrid, torn between Baroque and Classical instincts, which incidentally helps explain why music theorists have dithered about naming it. The Classical concerto could not escape the sonata principle, the force imbuing virtually all music in the Classical era. Reciprocity, like polarity, is a mode of concerto duality, and therefore reciprocity as an organizing principle is intrinsic to the genre. It is only one such principle, however. The other principle, sonata form, is not intrinsic.

We have already visited more than once the opening ritornello in ritornello sonata form and its reciprocal solo entry. Ordinarily replay is involved—replay at long distance (as in Example 7). The music that the solo replays was last heard two minutes ago when the piece began.

Let me stop for a moment and acknowledge that the idea of long-distance replay may give some listeners pause, to say nothing of remote counterplay: for there are indeed solo entries after a long ritornello that offer contrasting material, and the contention is that these are still heard in reference to the original music two minutes back. Memory is required, and memory of this kind is, I believe, developed by all listeners to classical music. One can enjoy a Mozart concerto without the application of such memory—one can enjoy a Mozart concerto in a dentist's chair or a Macy's elevator—but it takes memory to grasp its form. The importance of memory for the appreciation of music can hardly be overestimated.

Somewhat late in the day, let me also say that what may seem like undue solicitude in these conversations for musical form and principles of form comes from my conviction that form channels musical memory. It is not easy to remember music—to perceive music of any length as continuity—without some help from the markers of established form-templates (or at least of what James Hepokoski calls "deformations" of sonata form and the rest).[3] Conceiving form and continuity in this way underpins one of music criticism's most persistent and persistently controversial projects, that of reading music as some sort of story, or, more recently, mapping narrative theory onto music. To posit musical form as a mnemonic field with markers rather than a preset matrix for narrative might mute this controversy. (But this is not said to renounce or preclude narrative readings.)

We left the Classical concerto hanging at the point of solo entry, after the ritornello. As is well known, this entry triggers the exposition, also called the solo exposition, a large section of music that re-presents the ritornello material as a whole in a genial transformation. The solo, in cooperation with the orchestra, re-engages with that material and edits it, subtracting some bits, adding new bits of its own, modulating—an important function—altering the pace, and so on. All of this is heard, or can be heard, in reference to the ritornello itself. Reciprocity controls the whole exposition as well as the solo entry.

After this, however, sonata form comes into its own. As the concerto proceeds first to a development section and then to a recapitulation, like those of a symphony, solo/orchestra interplay is no longer functional. The concerto is now behaving like a symphony. The recapitulation, to be sure, links to the exposition by the same sort of musical memory that links the solo exposition to the ritornello. Memory in this case, however, does not work on anything reciprocal.

Ritornello sonata form also carried over somewhat awkwardly a relic from the Baroque era, namely two later ritornellos after the opening one that are still polarized. This was a feature that Mozart and Beethoven tended to modify (almost nullify), which is a long story that need not be told here. Let me take only a moment to look at the ways Mozart often arranged for some further reciprocal gestures, after the exposition section. In the accompanying diagrams, arrows show replays of earlier material in the solo exposition. Diagram 1 shows the default situation, as it is found in several of Mozart's Viennese piano concertos. A larger number of these works, however, also include a long-term replay in the recapitulation, of a theme from the ritornello that has been reserved and skipped over in the exposition (Diagram 2). Diagram 3 shows another similar idea. Finally, Diagram 4 records episodes from the long story that is not going to be told: Mozart rounding off the edges of a polarized second ritornello.

This formal feature in Mozart's concerto first movements has been much discussed and admired. If I have a contribution to make to this discussion, it would have to emerge from my view of reciprocity as one of the guiding principles of ritornello sonata form. What Mozart was doing may be seen as his response to an inexorable condition of this form, a form that submits only partly to an organizing principle that is intrinsic to the genre. Reciprocity guides its initial stages and loosens its hold later. In his sporadic and ad hoc fashion, Mozart was working to make Classical concerto form more reciprocal.

•✦ •✦ •✦

There is still more to say about Classical concerto form, which I defer until later. Right now I should like to shift to another area where reciprocity is all-important, that of concerto relationships.

Relationships between the concerto agents can be thought of in two ways, corresponding to two temporal dimensions, instantaneous and transient, vertical and horizontal, the domains of texture and (broadly speaking) form. The simplest of vertical relationships—they could be

Diagram 1   K. 413, 453, 456, 466

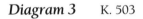

| Ritornello | *solo* | R | *solo* | *(recapitulation)* | R |

Diagram 2   K. 414, 415, 450, 459, 467, 491, 595

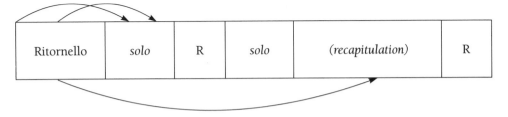

| Ritornello | *solo* | R | *solo* | *(recapitulation)* | R |

Diagram 3   K. 503

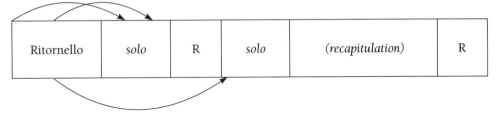

| Ritornello | *solo* | R | *solo* | *(recapitulation)* | R |

Diagram 4   K. 449, 451, 482, 488, 537

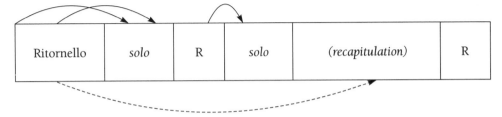

| Ritornello | *solo* | R | *solo* | *(recapitulation)* | R |

called immanent relationships—is solo melody accompanied by non-melody in the orchestra, that is, by chords or figuration or the like. Horizontal or dynamic relationships, on the other hand, are established over time: thus the orchestra makes a statement at one moment, and the next moment the solo answers it, or at some later time the solo recalls it, and so on. Such encounters, multiplied, add up to a relationship. It is obvious that dynamic relationships are predicated on reciprocity.

How to develop a criticism that can engage with the diverse qualities of concerto relationships? It will certainly be necessary to get past neutral terms like "accompany" and "answer," terms that are applied so routinely to musical events that they have lost their original figurative meaning, and might as well be technical terms like "chord" or "antecedent/consequent." Fresher tropes are needed, and it seems to me they have to be derived by analogy from human relationships (something commentators have been doing throughout the history of the concerto, as I have said a number of times). A concerto relationship can be playful, antagonistic, supportive, exploitative, and so on, and it can be many shades of the qualities indicated by these broad predicates.

I also like to think about and attempt to specify the roles that concerto agents assume, roles such as MASTER and SERVANT, or MENTOR and ACOLYTE. (When I was young, analogical or metaphorical efforts of this kind were taboo in academic music studies. The mandarin, Miltonian position was to dismiss such discourse as "incorrigible" and "literally meaningless." In today's musicology, though, meanings are discovered everywhere.) Among the roles that will be encountered later in these pages are EAVESDROPPER, TEASE, SURVIVOR, VICTIM, MOURNER or PLEURANT, MINX, LOVER, CRITIC, EDITOR . . . some of these, I suppose, will seem fanciful. Add roles authorized by the composers themselves: the forlorn Chatelaine of Carl Maria von Weber, Berlioz's Childe Harold, Richard Strauss's Don Quixote and Sancho Panza, and (as Owen Jander has argued at some length) Beethoven's Orpheus and the Furies.[4] Roles have already found their way into the present discussion: the NOSTALGIC of the Grieg Concerto, the generic EDITOR of ritornello sonata form, and the BOOSTER or BACK-SLAPPER of the mutual rondo.

In the Schumann Andante (see Example 19) the piano and the orchestra clearly assume the role of LOVERS. Robert wrote this concerto for Clara to concertize with soon after their marriage, so the *Liebe* in question is an altogether *eheliche Liebe,* conjugal love, as Beethoven would have put it.[5] (And the second theme in this movement, with its striding cello melody and fluttery piano responses, models the other, submissive side of the marital situation.)

Saint-Saëns' Cello Concerto in A minor provides a highly original example of role playing, in a passage that is also admirably calculated for the instrument. The piece is a continuous fast/medium tempo/fast structure, and in lieu of a slow movement the high strings dream up a delicate antique minuet. Its eight-bar phrases come to the appointed stop, whereupon the cello, entirely solo, muses slowly, starting with four long notes—a sphinx, Schumann would have called this, a sphinx that actually finds its way into the discourse. As the minuet resumes, the musing continues below, gently but more and more warmly, turning ultimately into a waltz . . . the soloist as EAVESDROPPER, like Berlioz's Childe Harold. He (not she, I think) is also a TIME-TRAVELER.

Example 20

In Example 17b, from the finale of the Brahms Piano Concerto No. 2, the piano makes a cameo appearance as TEASE (coplay! Brahms in a merry mood. He soon turns melancholy). Alban Berg, at the start of his Violin Concerto, introduces the orchestra and the violin as MENTOR and ACOLYTE; and since this mesmerizing passage may be read not merely as an Introduction, which is how Berg labels it in the score, but as a virtually all-encompassing birth metaphor—the birth of natural acoustics, birth of the violin, birth of the twelve-tone row, birth of Manon

Example 21

Gropius, birth of Woman—I also understand the role of the clarinet here as MIDWIFE.

It will be thought less fanciful, I hope, to identify at a later point in the Berg Concerto, at what the composer designated its *Höhepunkt*, a dramatic role change. The climax of the second movement has the full orchestra and solo hyperventilating in spasms of dissonant anguish; then they suddenly stop, and the violin turns to a Bach chorale, "Es ist genug." Although this is a chorale of consolation, the violin sings it not in belief but in dulled pain. The violin's role changes from DYING GIRL to PLEURANT, from Manon in death agony to grieving Alban.

A parallel can be drawn with *Wozzeck*. As the curtain comes down after the death of Wozzeck in Act III, the orchestra's role changes from that of DIRECTOR guiding or, really, driving the dramatic action to that of PLEURANT, once again—the same grieving Alban Berg. The lamentation pouring out of the pit during *Wozzeck*'s final orchestral interlude is no longer *of* the action, but *about* the action.[6]

*　·　·　·　·*

Roles can change with time—abruptly, as with Berg, or gradually. Relationships, too, change with time. When this happens purposefully over the course of an entire concerto, the composer has in effect constructed a narrative or, more correctly, a musical process that can be read as narrative. A *relationship story*, we could say.

Such a relationship story can be traced through the three movements of the Violin Concerto by Chaikovsky. This is a work of the sort that musicologists and some other people, too, tend to look down on as a solo "vehicle," with the solo engaged in solipsistic feats of virtuosity at the expense of an orchestra squelched into a mere SERVANT or SLAVE role. There is a lot of anxiety about virtuosity out there, in the traditional discourse on the concerto. Still, while the relationship may start out one-sided in the Chaikovsky concerto, it evolves in a striking way as the piece proceeds.

I have already spoken about the opening of this work, the orchestral introduction to the first movement, a mélange of attention-getting gestures, hints of the theme to come, and the rolling out of red carpets (see Example 3). Given a buildup like that, I said, the solo can enter like a prima donna with a flourish, a pirouette, and a self-serving mini-cadenza before singing her aria. The solo as DIVA, the orchestra as ADVANCE MAN. Thereafter throughout the entire exposition (for this movement is in sonata form) the solo domineers absolutely. The same thing happens in the recapitulation and the coda.

(One brief passage that may seem an exception I take to be the exception that proves the rule. In the bridge passage leading to the second theme, the orchestra and solo engage in a series of rapid alternations of a sort that had become a concerto cliché by Chaikovsky's time. The orchestral tutti introduces a quite decided motif to which the violin counterplays with solo scales or arpeggios, and this short composite unit is repeated and sequenced so as to achieve the key that the second theme requires. When this arrives, however, the solo wrests the motif from the orchestra. It was my music all the time, the violin seems to say.)

As for the middle of the movement, in between the exposition and the recapitulation: yes, the orchestra bursts in at last, as sooner or later it had to do, if only to allow the solo a break. And, on the assumption that the composer is working to project the relationship GENTLEWOMAN and SERVANT, or DIVA and DRESSER, or MISTRESS and SLAVE, an assumption that is unquestionably fomented by the orchestral introduction and the solo exposition, Chaikovsky's next move is ingenious: he brings the orchestra in strongly and then undermines it. He does this, in fact, twice.

The orchestra plays a martial theme—not a new theme, but a masculinized version of what I referred to as the violin's aria (Example 22a). The aria mutates into a polonaise, symbol of the courtly and the majestic, a marker of Chaikovsky's imperial style, as Richard Taruskin calls it (Example 22b).[7] Then the orchestra starts to develop the polonaise theme; the development section is getting under way. This composer's take on symphonic development in his Piano Concerto, and the generic critique implied by that work, have been spoken of above. Here, once again, development is sharply rejected by the solo, though in an almost opposite way from the Piano Concerto. The violin, after wagging her finger at the orchestra, settles in to a light-hearted, frilly variation of the orchestra's own theme—a rather startling evocation of the coloratura variations that were the staple of nineteenth-century divas, Jenny Lind singing variations on "The Last Rose of Summer," and the like (Example 22c). This place positively drips contempt for the orchestra's intellectual pretensions. The violin as MINX.

Example 22

The orchestra tries its polonaise again, is rejected again by the violin in a less amiable spirit, and is silenced by a premature cadenza. This prepares for the recapitulation. An attempt by the orchestra to lead comes to nothing. From this point on the movement returns to the MISTRESS/SERVANT situation once and for all.

Bringing in the cadenza at this point of the movement, and having it overlap the recapitulation, was an inspired idea of Mendelssohn's. Chaikovsky only pretends to give the orchestra (represented by its weakest member, the flute) its due and let it lead, for once, at this important place, with the main theme. The theme is deftly filched back at its most suggestive moment. The violin as CAD.

To be sure, there are different kinds of servants—Launcelot Gobbo,

Serpina, Uncle Tom, Jeeves . . . Chaikovsky's orchestra is a bit like Leporello, complaining loudly, and then put in its place.

‣ The relationship story takes a new turn in the second movement of Chaikovsky's Violin Concerto.

Like the first movement, the second also leads off with the orchestra, in effect with a ritornello. Played by winds alone, the strings silent, this rather somber, churchy music does not serve as an introduction, as in the first movement; it makes a cogent, self-contained, and functional statement. Yet the violin, with its polar entry, clearly has not heard this music. The first tune belongs entirely to the violin, and so does a second tune that appears in due course. A contemporary critic assured his readers that these melodies could not fail to remind them of women characters in Turgenev.

Track 6

Ritornello material returns in a beautiful passage following the second tune, after the violin has begun to spin out a winding line to make the retransition [2:48]. Up to this point the violin has been accompanied by strings, slavishly enough; now the woodwinds return, playing pungent French sixths. Almost unobtrusively they yield to sustained strings enunciating the original ritornello material [3:10]. The relationship—the immanent relationship—has begun to change, for the strings now sound in counterpoint to the violin's arabesque, rather than accompanying it. The wind music has been curtailed, shorn of its more distinctive harmonies and deprived of its sharper woodwind colors—in all, whitened. Music that had evoked some kind of monkish chanting when played by winds seems less song than discourse when played by the strings: sisterly, and secular. Meanwhile the violin obbligato becomes a little warmer, and a little faster, as though from a sense of recognition. The relationship has become dynamic. The two agents begin to engage.

And in the continuation, new possibilities of relationship open up in the alacrity with which the clarinet picks up the end of the violin's arabesque, and in the intimacy with which woodwinds echo the solo melody when it returns [3:35]. Veiled confidences between the solo winds and the violin seem also to presage a new covenant for the partitioned orchestra. At the end of the movement winds and strings finally come together and make the transition to the finale [5:24]. Important things are now happening without the solo; in this impressive passage the violin plays no part.

·⤳ Segue to the finale, Allegro vivacissimo, with its brilliant and marvelously intricate first theme. Synergy between discourse and display never gets better than this. Once again the solo takes full possession. Track 7 Though it feels as unstoppable as in the first movement, in fact it *is* stopped, or at any rate, slowed. This happens during the second theme, when the orchestra replays music that has just been played by the solo [2:21].

This is so ordinary an occurrence, so banal—yet this is the first time it has happened in the whole of the composition. The orchestra in fact replays and replays and replays; a series of minuscule variations emerges, played by the two concerto agents on a surprisingly equitable basis. The orchestra is unusually expansive and inventive. It generates a wealth of textures and colors—the tune in airy high strings grounded by a syncopated bass, with the violin in the middle; the tune in the French horns; then the tune in the basses. New fireworks light up the sky in the recapitulation of this passage, later: high flutes doubled below by violin double stops; a backbeat in pizzicato chords; French horns again; then lightly chromatic woodwind counterpoints . . . up to a variation of a different and much more surprising kind [2:39].

Many things surprise here. There is the Molto meno mosso indication, which slows down the seemingly unstoppable—slows the tempo by just about a half; the fact that it is the orchestra that does the slowing; the change in mode from major to minor; and the very strange mood, both lazy and somehow sly. The minor mode invites complexity, and the theme is subjected to a process of sophistication in melody, harmony, and form. The orchestra analyzes the theme by shaping its constituent phrases, subtly differentiating them, and allocating them to different, dialoguing instruments.

This is another generic critique, then, like the confrontation in the middle of the first movement. Though what was edgy there is here controlled and ironic. Chaikovsky is unpacking the popular ethnic tone found so often in concerto finales: a hornpipe in Handel's Concerto Grosso in B-flat, Opus 6 No. 11, a mazurka in Chopin's F-minor Concerto, echoes of Russian folk-dances called *naigrïshi*, of the kind popularized by Glinka's orchestral fantasia *Kamarinskaya*, in this work of his own.[8] In a notorious review that Chaikovsky never forgot, Eduard Hanslick railed against the "miserable, trivial Cossack cheer" in Chaikovsky's finale, claiming that the piece taught him something he had never known before, namely that music could actually stink. Yet Hanslick knew perfectly well that his much-admired Brahms wrote finales with an explicit ethnic accent. Brahms furnished his First Piano Concerto and his Violin Concerto with Hungarian finales, neither of which drops so much as a hint of reflection or irony.

(Another passage a little later in Chaikovsky's finale deserves a moment's attention. When orchestral exclamations of a motif taken from the first theme alternate with strenuous violin double stops, at closer and closer time intervals, the music recalls the episode of orchestra-solo alternations in the bridge of the first movement. This time things do not come out to the advantage of the soloist. The orchestra enjoys a little burst of assertion at the end, and the solo changes the subject, as it were, by starting a new train of events in the low register. On the other hand, when this passage of alternations returns to initiate the coda, the violin takes back some of the action.)

We have come a long way: from the orchestra as SLAVE to the orchestra as CRITIC. After three movements, the agents have reached a point where there is genuine give and take between them, very different from the formal introductions and staged confrontations of the first movement, different also from the moving, ambiguous intimacies of the second. The agents are on the verge, at least, of a new easy, open relationship. We could call it emancipated.

·~ ·~ ·~

This has been one relationship story. Another can be read in Beethoven's Piano Concerto No. 4 in G major, as I have recounted elsewhere.[9] Another story, more generalized—more myth than narrative—has been adumbrated in the discussion a little while ago of reciprocity and concerto forms. That discussion was admittedly rather abstract, and the general sense or quality of ritornello sonata form and the mutual rondo may come clearer if they can be considered in context, that is, as elements in a total three-movement form.

The three-movement Classical concerto, and this is something I mooted some years ago, can be read in terms of the underlying theme of comedy, expounded by Northrop Frye, for example, as the "myth of spring."[10] Others have said something similar, eloquent among them my colleague Wye J. Allanbrook. In brief: the subject, uncertain of its place in the world, undergoes various tests, hazards, and misadventures; but all turns out well, and the individual is finally welcomed into society. And thereby society is transformed. I was thinking of Mozart, of course, and in fact with Mozart this mirrors an actual social dynamic in the years 1782 to 1786, when he wrote the majority of his piano concertos for the *Akademien* he put on in order to establish himself in Vienna as a freelance musician. The myth is explicit in *The Magic Flute* as well. In the opera Tamino plays the flute, I wrote; in seventeen concertos Amadeus plays the fortepiano.

What he plays always falls into three stages, the three acts of an eighteenth-century high comedy. In the first act, in ritornello sonata form, the concerto agents enter into a collaborative test situation. The individual presents himself to the group and shows how he can cope with conditions they have laid down in the opening ritornello. Mediated by dialogue, the relationship develops as the conditions change, for the orchestra allows and even invites criticism, initiative, and spontaneous display on the part of the soloist.

Act II, the slow middle movement, sometimes records the trials and tribulations of the subject. (Example 18 shows the denouement of one such piece.) More often the slow movement is a quiet interlude—lyric, idyllic, Utopian. These interludes are less easy to "read" in terms of a narrative; perhaps one could say that whereas in the tragic or pathetic slow movements the individual has lived through his dark hour, in the idyllic movements a ritual of communal acceptance has been solemnized between the principals. Then comes a rondo (usually), and here less is at stake than in the initial sustained encounter. The mutual rondo of Act III is nothing like a trial or a quest. It celebrates achievement, acceptance, alliance. The relationship between solo and orchestra is less like collaboration than complicity.

The three movements of the Classical concerto trace a sequence, then, from interaction to respite, or occasionally passion, to alliance. The actors move from collaborative and creative exchange to accommodation. The forms of the individual movements play into the form of the whole, and if I may return to my earlier theme, the phases of interaction and alliance, at least, are assuredly determined by reciprocity. As these are the outer corners of the total form, it is right to understand reciprocity as the main organizing principle for the Classical concerto as a whole.

Virtuosity / Virtù   *4*

"The crucial moment for establishing the nature of the tutti-solo relationship," writes Jane R. Stevens, a historian of the concerto in the eighteenth century, in a recent 800-page book of essays on the Mozart piano concertos, "is perhaps the solo's entrance at the beginning of the first solo section."[1] That is a large claim, even though the word "perhaps" is always a great safety valve, and it struck me particularly because I was within an inch of making some such claim myself in the first of these concerto conversations. Even so, even failing that, remarks on that occasion will have left you with the idea that getting started in concertos bears more than anecdotal interest. Sometimes the solo entry can foretell or drive the music that is to come, as well as just initiating it. In such cases the entry deserves, perhaps, to be called crucial.

This appears to be the case always—no perhapses—with dialogue entries in concertos, a category mentioned but hurried past in previous lectures. Yet surely the most radical and at the same time the most characteristic way of starting a concerto is with active conversation between solo and orchestra. It does not happen very often. Returning to this topic briefly, before moving on to discuss virtuosity, I can perhaps pull together some loose ends from Lecture 1 and also Lecture 3, "Reciprocity, Roles, and Relationships"—Stevens speaks specifically about relationship.

One loose end was left by my reference to the opening of Alban Berg's Violin Concerto, with its unforgettable up-and-down arpeggios for clarinets, harp, and violin. That was a dialogue entry, an initiation; with the agents in the relationship of MENTOR and ACOLYTE, the orchestra offers its precept four times, and each time the violin accepts, absorbs, and expands the precept by means of replay. For Berg, this was a way of thematizing dialogue right away, and in particular, thematizing replay—not a very usual phenomenon for a twentieth-century concerto, but a feature of this one. The medley of Mahlerian waltzes in the first movement is presented almost always in orchestra-violin replay. The Bach chorale introduced in the second movement, also in replay, or coplay, brings back the original dialogists, violin and clarinets, with a piercing effect.

It is probably clear that I am taking "dialogue entry" to mean something more than a single reciprocal exchange between solo and orchestra at the beginning of a concerto, as happens famously in Beethoven's Piano Concerto No. 4 and differently if equally famously in Mozart's early Piano Concerto in E-flat, K. 271. Both of Mendelssohn's piano concertos start with a more protracted, developing interchange. Where Beethoven had started with an oracle, and Mozart with a prank, Mendelssohn in his Piano Concerto No. 2 in D minor plunges immediately into an evolving drama, a relationship at work.

Example 23

Or at least a melodrama. The opening orchestral statement, first gloomy, then agitated, is met by a sympathetic counterplay from the piano in quasi-recitative, which heats up as the conversation proceeds. The movement's first theme grows out of the orchestral complex. To nobody's surprise, when this returns as a recapitulation (without the piano response), the gloom has intensified into high distress; and in the coda, distress erupts into something like frenzy. Woodwinds have to mediate between the orchestra and the solo. The ultimate solo reponse is a replay, not a counterplay. The piano sings of an almost overpowering gentleness and in fact transcendence, for the coda becomes more than a coda. It forms a quiet and yet quite emphatic transition into the slow movement, one of Mendelssohn's most beautiful.

Mendelssohn was putting the dialogue entry to work here for the total form of the concerto, which he was trying as always to make more fluid and less monumental than in his Classical models. During the first half of the nineteenth century Weber, Schumann, Liszt, and almost every other serious writer of concertos was moving in this same direction. (The Piano Concerto in A minor by Clara Wieck, 1835, a fairly recent arrival in the record stores, illustrates this tendency in a striking way.) The first movement created a special problem for these composers, and in both Mendelssohn piano concertos he made use of dialogue first to loosen up the beginning of the necessarily somewhat intense first movement, and then again as a way of leading this Allegro smoothly, without a heavy stop—and without a cadenza—into a more relaxed Andante.

Things proceed differently in the First Piano Concerto of Liszt, who, now that he has found his way into our conversation with his dazzling exhibition of concerto dialogue, will not leave it willingly. The opening exchange heats up, all right—if not sequentially, as with Mendelssohn, in seemingly disconnected waves or bursts. Where Mendelssohn is logical, Liszt is impulsive and erratic. While Liszt's conversation emanates from the Romantic theater, Mendelssohn's seems overheard during some Victorian domestic altercation. The opening orchestral challenge in the Liszt—it could almost be quoted from a drama by Victor Hugo— promises confrontation. In a first response, the piano hurls the orchestra's modulation back, and then proceeds to pick the challenge apart in

Track 8

a short cadenza [0:33]. In a second response, when the orchestra re-peats its challenge, suitably chastened, it meets with passionate remon-stration from the piano [1:01, 1:23—most passionate of all at 4:19]. The dialogue will ultimately drift into a dreamlike pleasure garden where solo clarinets and violins assume the roles of Flower Maidens [1:49]; the piano itself has switched roles from HERNANI to KUNDRY. The third response comes some time later, after the solo and the orchestra have awakened from the dream. The orchestra delivers its challenge with new emphasis and bluster; the piano snatches its theme and runs it furiously down the keyboard to closure [3:28]. Liszt here resumes his trademark bravura double octaves, first heard in the original piano response.

As in Mendelssohn, this elaborate, drawn-out dialogue entry plays into the form of the whole.[2] The orchestra's challenge, together with one or more of the solo responses, returns at some length in the center of the work and also provides it with the by now obligatory rousing con-clusion. Unlike most of the other musical material, the entry music does not undergo Liszt's familiar transformation process. It serves as a sort of motto or naive leitmotif—not a leitmotif of the fully developed kind, but the kind used in *Lohengrin,* the latest Wagner opera known to Liszt when he completed his two concertos in the 1850s. Well known: Liszt had recently presided over *Lohengrin's* first performance.

.⌣ .⌣ .⌣

And who better than Liszt to lead us into the topic of this lecture, which is virtuosity? The first thing to say about virtuosity is that true virtuos-ity requires no apology. I say "true virtuosity" because listening to flawed virtuosity is like watching college football—a site of empathy and rapture for fans and alumni, but noplace on the scale of aesthetic experience. The real thing, on the other hand, is something one can't have enough of . . .

At this point in the lecture video clips were shown of Joan Sutherland, singing coloratura passages from Bellini and the cadenza to "Je suis Titania" from Mignon, *by Ambroise Thomas.*

Needless to say, and with all due respect to Liszt, the choice of a vocal excerpt on this occasion was a calculated choice. That the human voice is the model for musical instruments is a truism, but it is a profound truism, and without it no consideration of the concerto could proceed very far. Earlier I called melodies in Chaikovsky's Violin Concerto arias and songs—so ordinary a locution that it was probably hardly noticed; and Chaikovsky too, when he entitled his second movement "Canzonetta," probably didn't give it a minute's thought.

Indeed—to pick up another thread—-the voice/instrument equation lies behind concerto ritornello form, a subject that keeps coming up in these conversations. The grand operatic aria provided the direct model for this form. That same 800-page volume on Mozart concertos includes an essay, by Martha Feldman, showing how the ritornello form of Mozart's Salzburg violin concertos is patterned on certain of his opera arias; and what's new about this is not the basic idea—Donald Tovey in a classic essay derived concerto form from the big bravura aria in *Die Entführung aus dem Serail,* "Martern aller Arten"—but the author's demonstration of how astonishingly literal Mozart's derivation was.[3]

(One more word, though, about ritornello forms in vocal and instrumental music: for all their kinship, there is a fundamental difference. With the reciprocal solo entry after a ritornello in an aria, *words* are heard, words that articulate the affect of the ritornello's music—and by doing so, put the ritornello in a subsidiary, because derivative, position. The words reveal it as heretofore an incomplete, tentative thing awaiting realization. In a concerto, the ritornello is realized at the start, once and for all. The opening ritornello material is primary and lays down the conditions for the solo entry. In an aria, it's the solo entry that is primary, and that has merely been adumbrated by the ritornello. The first is a case of solo replay, the second a case of orchestral foreplay.)

Moreover, it is really only the status of instruments as vocal surrogates that justifies the so-common analogy between the agents of a concerto and human agents. The analogy holds even though a musical instrument is human only insofar as it is an extension of the body, like a spade or a distaff, while voice is body itself, like an eye or an arm. More than an arm, more even than the eye, voice is the expression of self within the body.

That is why when people thrill to virtuoso singing, they also relate to a body and merge, sometimes, with a self or with a represented operatic self. We do something of the same kind in response to an instrumental virtuoso. We do the same in response to an athlete: an analogy that goes back to the Olympic Games and need cause musicians not the least discomfort. The same lift, the same ecstasy can come from witnessing an individual do something superbly well, something we know is difficult and dangerous, and something we could not do ourselves. This must be as fundamental an aesthetic experience as taking in a tune, let alone enjoying a musical dialogue.

Display and discourse—both primary components of the aesthetic of the concerto.

. ._ ._ ._

If virtuosity is primary, then, and if virtuosity needs no apology, why bring up apology in the first place? Because when virtuosity is not being run down in the literature, it is usually being apologized for. To take a random and thoroughly banal example from a current book called *A Guide to the Concerto,* one of those depressing if necessary manuals that deliver scraps of fact and opinion about hundreds of art works, more than anyone will ever hear or want to hear—this *Guide* offers a total of five terse sentences about the once-popular Violin Concerto No. 2 by Henryk Wieniawski, which according to sentence no. 1 is "often called his finest work." Sentence no. 2 says something or other, and then no. 3 says of the first movement: "Despite passages of brilliance . . . one never feels that virtuosity is the *raison d'être* of the work." And after sentence no. 4 has checked off the slow movement, the last sentence reads: "The finale, *Allegro molto, alla Zingara*—in other words, in gypsy style—is energetic but again not excessive in display."[4]

The British art of damning with faint praise. Virtuosity is here equated with brilliance and display, and the second thing to say about virtuosity is that it cries out to be construed more broadly. While in musical discourse "virtuosity" is usually taken to mean bravura, no more than bravura, performers do other things supremely well—and are admired for it—besides the execution of bravura. In non-musical discourse the word *virtuosity* has been borrowed from us and stretched; we read of "verbal virtuosity," "virtuoso diplomacy," and even "the greatest virtuoso in the field of hypnosis"—the latter from that old reliable writers' best friend, the *OED.* Rather than stretching the term, I mean to replace it by a more ecumenical relative: not virtue, which has moral associations that I do not fancy, but the naturalized Italian *virtù,* which has Machiavellian credentials that I rather do. A secondary meaning of virtù, power or capability, is stronger in Italian than in English, where it survives mainly in locutions such as "by virtue of the authority granted in me . . ." And there is no question that the musician's expertise is the result of long practice and the most careful calculation.

Given the solo's role as PRINCE, then, what constitutes its virtù? Most of what will be proposed now applies obviously to vocal as much as to instrumental performance, and to instruments generally, not only to instruments in their roles as concerto soloists. But what applies to instruments generally applies *a fortiori* to concerto soloists; individual virtù makes its effect most strongly in a wider context, by means of contrast with a group. In the Liszt E-flat Concerto, for example, surely the virtuoso octaves at 3:28 sound even more brilliant coming as they do after the orchestral explosion (Track 8).

The musician's virtù has, I would say, three aspects or components. They are bravura, mimesis, and spontaneity, expressed in improvisation. Bravura means playing at the very edge of technique, at risk, what one scarcely imagined could be played: very fast music, unexpectedly loud music, high music for voices and instruments other than keyboard instruments, string double stops, harmonics, and bariolage, non-stop music and multiphonics for wind instruments, and more. Virtuosity, as I have already said, is often taken to be no more than bravura.

Mimesis probably does not come to mind at once as an element of musical virtù (*pace* Vivaldi and "The Four Seasons" . . . though perhaps with their hundred-plus entries in the Schwann Catalogue these pieces never *are* silent). Imitation of the sounds of nature counts for less than the imitation of other musical instruments. The piano can mimic a music box, in the Chaikovsky Piano Concerto, or it can simulate the awesome bells of Hell, in Liszt's *Totentanz*, or a full orchestra, in almost any late-nineteenth-century warhorse. The audience is elated by the performer's tiny art, or agreeably scared out of its skins, or astounded by the instrument's unbelievable range and power.

The violin can evoke trumpet fanfares—a regular stylistic feature in Vivaldi, traceable to a Bolognese tradition of trumpet concertos, perhaps—or a flamenco guitar, in Benjamin Britten's Violin Concerto, or a shepherd's pipe, in Beethoven's Violin Concerto. Later an oboe clarifies the pastoral reference; later still, in a certain other work actually entitled "Pastoral," the reference is spelled out.

Example 24

What counts for the most of all is imitation of the human voice. We are back to voice: voice as lyric song, voice as declamation, voice as lament—and for that matter, voice as shriek and groan. But principally voice as the wellspring of melody. Nobody doubts that projecting melody in an affecting way counts as a central component of any musician's equipment, although once again, this is not usually spoken of as virtuosity (which is why I am using the word *virtù*).

Instrumental mimesis of lament will be taken up at some length in the last of these lectures. Mimesis of vocal declamation inspires passages such as one from the slow movement of the Second Clarinet Concerto by Carl Maria von Weber, marked Recitativo. At the end of the movement, this declamation gives way to a lovely lyric recapitulation—recitative gives way to aria or arioso.[5] And my third attribute of

Example 25

voice, lyric melody, is what musicians think of first when they think of voice. All instruments try to sing, even unlikely ones: brass instruments (of which at least the trombone would have been considered unlikely before the age of jazz); plucked instruments (the guitar, acoustic and electric); and keyboard instruments like the harpsichord, the piano, and the organ, in Handel's organ concertos.

In Handel's time, and in Mozart's, imitating human song meant imitating the ornaments and graces that singers regularly applied to melody lines that were notated in a skeletal form, in a sort of shorthand. Embellishment is surely essential—or anyhow, something has to be done—in order to maintain the illusion that a keyboard instrument can sing. Handel marks certain passages in his concertos "ad libitum" to assure improvised ornamentation. On the other hand, Artur Schnabel in a classic series of Mozart concerto recordings doggedly played the slow-movement cantilena exactly according to the shorthand of the original score, skeletal lines almost entirely devoid of ornaments. It would make a fascinating digression—one that could not be justified for this occasion—to inquire into why this great artist went so wrong, why so many listeners have loved it, and why his literalism has been followed by so many pianists and even fortepianists up to the present day. In the eighteenth century, the virtù of the performer was shown expressly by his art of improvised ornamentation. There are recordings today displaying ornaments (and cadenzas) that have been improvised in the recording studio—Mozart recordings by Chick Corea, a master of today's preeminent school of improvisation, jazz; and Mozart and Beethoven recordings by Robert Levin, who has recreated, and is constantly recreating, the art as it was in those composers' times.[6] A cadenza improvised by Levin can be heard on Track 1, 12:36.

From early times, as is well known, ornamentation was sometimes written out rather than applied *ex tempore*—either improvised and then remembered on paper, or else composed on paper in what would be recognized as an improvisatory style. A useful formula for this discussion is "improvised or improvisatory." (There exists a manuscript with such ornaments to a Mozart Concerto—the A major, K. 488—in the hand of his pupil Barbara Ployer; unfortunately, it goes some way to justify the homilies on bad taste invariably found in eighteenth-century writings on ornamentation.)[7] Chopin was one of the last improvisers in the great tradition, and the exquisite ornamentation that is written out for the slow-movement themes of his concertos is not improvised, obviously, but improvisatory.

After Chopin, ornamentation soon went out of fashion, sooner in instrumental music than in opera. Limpid simplicity was in. Both of the Mendelssohn piano concertos and his Violin Concerto feature bare, ostensibly artless tunes in their slow movements, evoking the simplest

of Lieder, Songs without Words. The slow-movement tune in Chai- kovsky's Piano Concerto is even plainer. A child could play it. It may be
suspected that the studied *semplicità* of this particular melody pays
mistaken homage to Chaikovsky's idol, that same Mozart who wrote the
bare skeletal lines played by Schnabel—shorthand writing, outlines for
improvised or improvisatory ornamentation.

Example 26

The third aspect or constituent of musical virtù, spontaneity, manifests
itself both in ornamentation and in a larger-scale activity: that of improvising quantities of music from scratch and at length, not bound to an
already existing melodic line. Music of this sort—improvised or improvisatory—goes under many names: toccata, fantasia, prelude, perfidia,
fugue (the improvisation of fugues was a special mark of an organist's
virtù; organ recitals still sometimes feature improvised fugues on a
subject solicited from the audience), and *cadenza,* the concerto name.
The concern here is not so much with the nature of the improvisation
in any individual cadenza as with the role of the cadenza in the course
of the work as a whole.

I have made much of the importance of the solo entry in a concerto,
and have quoted Jane Stevens to this effect in reference to eighteenth-
century practice in particular. The solo *exit* is very important also—for
inasmuch as the orchestra is going to have the final say, the solo needs
all the more to make an effect with its last statement. Hence the final
cadence for the solo, before the orchestra comes in to wrap up the
proceedings, became the main juncture for virtuosity, in concerto as in
opera. What began as an embellished and thereby emphasized cadence
evolved into a flourish, then into an extended array of flourishes, and
then into the cadenza proper. A considerable span of music, the cadenza came to include not only bravura—ultimate bravura, quite liter-

ally—but references to the themes of the movement, modulations, and other phenomena that seem less and less like display and more and more like fractured discourse.

It is clear that from the earliest days of the concerto, performers have sometimes, or often, taken advantage of the aporia that is the solo's final cadence as a moment of carnival. This is the last chance for solo display, free of orchestral constraints—for orchestral discourse has simply stopped, and applause will soon be coming. (Concerto soloists need applause. Though virtue is said to be its own reward, no one ever said that about virtuosity.) Embellishment for the purpose of emphasis merges into extravagance and extravagance into transgression. Those who have seen the film *Farinelli* will remember a literally devastating cadenza for soprano and trumpet.

Some extravagant cadenzas were committed to paper, such as the well-known cadenza for harpsichord in Bach's Brandenburg Concerto No. 5. The composer wrote this out twice, the second, more brilliant version appearing in the presentation copy for the Margrave of Brandenburg. Bach also transcribed for keyboard a written-out cadenza by Vivaldi, a fine eruption of Baroque bravura (it was evidently portable, appearing in manuscripts of Vivaldi's D-major violin concertos RV 208 and RV 562; the Bach work is Organ Concerto No. 5 in C, BWV 594). In the Classical concerto, the distention of cadential energy that is promoted by the cadenza is, at the very least, unclassical—to say nothing of the license granted by improvisation, the license to break with tempo and rhythm, recall themes, make modulations, and what not, indifferent to the balance of theme and tonality in the work as a whole. From the standpoint of musical discourse, the cadenza is a disruption, a poltergeist in the stately home of Classical music. "The saddest chapter in the story of the concerto," intoned Tovey, whose luminous and still essential writings on the concerto focused so narrowly on the ideals and standards of Classicism.[8] Tovey was not one to enjoy the cadenza as an ostentatious parenthesis in the course of a concerto movement. For him it was an aleatoric alibi for a crucial element in the form, namely the coda. Hence his own published efforts at writing cadenzas for some of the great Classical masterpieces, in order (he said) to supply them with plausible codas on the Beethovenian model.

What Tovey admired (and played, as a performer) were the cadenzas left by Mozart. Probably written out for the benefit of students, these admirable cadenzas are concise, tactful, impeccable, Classical. Yet it is hard to believe that what Mozart actually played at his subscription concerts did not draw much more from the spirit of carnival. The character of this composer presented by Peter Shaffer in *Amadeus* has been deplored, yet there is evidence for it, or for one aspect of it, as in a memoir by Karoline Pichler, then young and later a prominent Viennese bluestocking and the poet of a few Schubert songs.

> Once when I was sitting at the piano playing "Non più andrai" from *Figaro*, Mozart, who happened to be with us, . . . pulled up a chair, sat down, told me to continue playing the bass and began to improvise such wonderfully beautiful variations that everyone present held his breath, listening to the music of the German Orpheus. But then he suddenly tired of it, jumped up, and, in the silly mood that so often came over him, began jumping over tables and chairs, meowing like a cat, and turning somersaults like a disorderly brat.[9]

It is in that meowing, bratty mood that I like to think of Mozart improvising his cadenzas—I like to think that was one way he held his audience.

Another unbuttoned character was Beethoven; the concept of cadenza as transgression is most familiar to us (and to Tovey) from the written-out cadenzas by this composer. These cadenzas were written years later than the earliest of the concertos, and by this time

Beethoven's idea of piano bravura and—not coincidentally—the instrument itself had progressed far. The cadenzas fairly blow the early music apart. They play considerable havoc (in one case, at least) with Piano Concerto No. 4, and reach vintage carnival status in a four-and-a-half-minute cadenza for the Violin Concerto, which among other things brings back the concerto's signature timpani together with an entirely new military march. (Beethoven transcribed the Violin Concerto for piano and orchestra, and while the cadenza is preserved only in the piano version, it is clear that he originally meant it for violin.[10] The march, by the way, turns up again approximately in *Fidelio.* Drums turn up again in cadenzas for the Beethoven composed by Busoni and Schnittke.)

And after that, after committing to paper some of the most untrammeled cadenzas on record, Beethoven turned around and virtually killed the cadenza, in the first movement of the "Emperor" Concerto. As is always observed, however, Beethoven did compensate for this near-kill by writing out a series of improvisatory bravura passages at the very start of the movement (Track 2). The same series returns at the point of recapitulation. Later, within one of those typically grandiose passages whipped up by an orchestra to signal the advent of a cadenza, the improvisatory piano gestures arrive again for the third time, in a much compressed form. But then, after all this preparation, the cadenza (which is all written out, such as it is, in the score) dissipates; French horns from the orchestra quietly co-opt it, and thereafter the orchestra is back to stay. The movement ends with piano and orchestra together. It is the first concerto movement to end with the characteristic "heroic" coda that Beethoven had perfected in symphonies, quartets, and sonatas.

Diagrams on page 49 showed how Mozart planned long-distance effects of reciprocity; this place in the "Emperor" must count as the most stunning such effect in concerto history. (I count it as reciprocal because of the lovely piano tracery accompanying the French horns. Previously the horns had played this theme alone.) The sublime surprise of it all is heightened by the fact that the cadenza undercut by the horns has been proceeding so normally, with an almost mandatory reference to the second theme—one would give odds that after four bars the little march will sequence up to F-sharp minor . . .

·◡ ·◡ ·◡

I have lingered on this very familiar passage from Beethoven because it really does count as a watershed moment in the history of the cadenza. Less and less in the nineteenth century does the performer show off his or her virtù by spontaneity in cadenza playing, any more than in melodic ornamentation. Composers either leave out those pompous orchestral signaling passages so that there is no place for a cadenza at all (Weber, Chopin, Mendelssohn in his piano concertos), or they write out their own obligatory cadenzas (Mendelssohn in his Violin Concerto, Schumann, Liszt, Chaikovsky, Rachmaninoff, and on).

Brahms, typically enough, maintains or goes back to the Classical procedure and provides a place for a cadenza that is to be supplied by the virtuoso performer—albeit in only one of his concertos, the Violin Concerto, and there only because the original performer was his close friend, the violinist-composer Joseph Joachim. (Joachim wrote out his cadenza; Tovey rewrote it.) Brahms himself took care of the cadenza for the finale, and entered it into the score. Szymanowsky did the same thing with cadenzas for both of his violin concertos supplied by the violinist Paul Kochánski.

Cadenzas are now no longer always written in an improvisatory style. How could they be, when improvisation no longer exists as a current practice? More and more, cadenzas form an integral part of the total discourse of their concertos. Tovey was swimming with the tide after all. Cadenzas, bravura and all, can become as functional as any other formal element or unit. Sometimes they are still labeled "cadenza," sometimes not. No longer transgressive, no longer carnivalesque, they are set apart from the rest of the discourse by affording the solo a private place, as it were, from which he or she can address the audience more directly, perhaps more intimately, rather than working with and through the orchestra.

A case in point is the back-breaking or at any rate bridge-breaking cadenza in the Berg Violin Concerto. This four-part canon could hardly be called improvisatory, and it does not bear the designation "cadenza," but with the orchestra silent, the violin can recall nostalgic music from earlier in the work in a way reminiscent of traditional cadenza action. It recalls it in an extraordinarily clear-eyed way, at the same time as it functions, I think, as a herald of deepening contrapuntal textures in the concluding chorale complex.

One could adduce many other instances of cadenzas incorporated into the total discursive structure of their hosts, all in quite different ways. In Rachmaninoff's Piano Concerto No. 1, the lyrical main theme is always marked *mf* until the cadenza, where, just before the end of the first movement, the piano thunders the theme out in a great fortissimo. The cadenza here works as an apotheosis. Equally functional (and more interesting) is the cadenza apotheosis in Rachmaninoff's Third Concerto; this moment also counts as an apotheosis of bravura.

Possibly influenced by the older composer, Prokofiev in his Piano Concerto No. 2 in G minor turns the cadenza to highly original use. The first movement falls into a pattern that would also serve the composer in his Violin Concerto No. 1—a work we shall be looking at later—and elsewhere. A leisurely melody is followed by a contrasting section (a parody gavotte: a Prokofiev signature), followed by the original melody in a heightened guise. In the piano concerto the return of the original melody is a 70-bar piano solo. What starts as a note-for-note return, surrounded by very many other notes in improbable clusters, simultaneous scales, and arpeggios, is slowly overtaken by bravura, as the music gets louder and louder and freer and freer. Toward the end, in a typical improvisatory ploy, previous themes or motifs are combined to add contrapuntal intensity to the shattering rampage of piano sound (the dotted-note incipit figure in Example 27 sounding above and below the slower ascending scale). A mighty cadenza has been made to grow seamlessly out of a major thematic return.

Example 27

Also original in its much quieter way is Aaron Copland's Concerto for Clarinet, one of his most urbane and engaging compositions. Using a cadenza as a transition linking movements is not an uncommon procedure, in fact common with some composers (such as Shostakovich. A precedent of sorts can be glimpsed in the Third Brandenburg Concerto). But whereas most cadenzas look back to earlier thematic material, Copland looks ahead: the cadenza that follows his opening slow movement introduces thematic fragments that will coalesce into real themes in the jazzy fast movement to come. The cadenza here works as gestation or, as Benny Goodman, who commissioned the piece, might have preferred to say, as creative noodling.

One last example, from an Introduction and Allegro for Piano and Orchestra by Robert Schumann, Opus 134, possibly the first movement of a planned concerto—a late work, composed shortly before his commitment, but by no means to be dismissed on that account. This movement incidentally features a dialogue entry, like those discussed earlier, except that the orchestra can hardly raise its voice above a whisper throughout. The whole piece stays uncommonly close to its tonic key

*Plate 4. Benny Goodman with Charles Munch and
the Boston Symphony Orchestra*

of D minor, introducing serious harmonic contrast at only one place—within the cadenza, a lengthy plateau of non-improvisatory sound entirely in B major. The cadenza here works as a vision of Utopia.

.⌣ .⌣ .⌣

I must now yield the conversation back—reasonably enough, I hope—to Liszt, though not on account of the cadenzas in his piano concertos, which are many, but quite short and surely not integrated into any larger discourse. With Liszt, what feels improvised is the form—the whole score, piano and orchestra together. Let us remember the formula "improvised or improvisatory." While characterizing a written-out score as improvisatory might seem paradoxical or perverse, it should seem less so in view of the quite massive available evidence of written-out ornamentation and written-out cadenzas. Liszt provides the illusion of the improvisation of form, an ostensibly extemporaneous sequence of themes, transitions, responses, actions, events, initiatives, recollections, and so on.

In this respect his Second Piano Concerto, in A major, is more extreme than the First, in E-flat—though one can surely sense improvisation in the beginning section of the E-flat Concerto discussed earlier (Track 8). Cursory analysis of the A-major work reveals many aberrant features which at the very least go against traditional precepts of musical composition. After the first few bars, given to the woodwinds, a clarinet emerges with a little cadenza, as though Liszt were not quite sure who was going to be the soloist. A little later a striking French horn reverie starts up and then drops out of sight forever. In its second appearance, a forceful *Mazeppa*-like section, bearing the inscription *"scharf markirt und abgestossen,"* brings with it three rather urgent fragments of melody and again, these never return—which is to say, never jell with the rest of the discourse. The piano, playing its bravura double octaves, concludes the piece with an entirely fresh transformation of an earlier theme—a spur-of-the-moment inspiration, or so it seems, just about twenty seconds before the end.

A passage from the middle of the A-major Concerto can illustrate how Liszt makes his melodic expansions sound spontaneous, casual, and innocently inventive. The thematic work in the piano here consists Example 28 largely of short, even phrases in sequence, phrases that are stronger on enthusiastic thrust than on thematic logic. Developing variation it is not; you can see why the young Brahms nodded off listening to this sort of thing at his only-too-memorable visit to Liszt in 1850. But Brahms doesn't sound improvisatory. Liszt does, I think, exactly because of his absent-mindedness and his imprecision, and also because of a formulaic quality which, in most true improvisations, is more rather than less in evidence.

One important result of all this—or was it really a precondition?—is that the Liszt concertos break down, or eschew, traditional concerto forms and traditional musical forms of any kind. "Break down" is the right term for the First Concerto, in E-flat, where shards of a nocturne and of a scherzo can still be detected; "eschew" is a better term for the Second. The A-major Concerto moves continuously without any stop from one short section to the next—slow, fast, very slow, very fast, *markirt, appassionato,* or *con abbandono.* In this matter Liszt marched in the advance guard of a general movement: all serious composers in the first half of the nineteenth century were seeking freer forms than that of the Classical three-movement model, as I have remarked before. Liszt went further than any of them, much further, further even than later composers who admired his achievement and tried to emulate it in their own work: such as the feeble Piano Concerto in C-sharp minor by Rimsky-Korsakov actually dedicated to Liszt, or Saint-Saëns' single big effort along these lines, Piano Concerto No. 4 in C minor, a work which simply cannot shed its Mendelssohnian allegiances.

In an earlier lecture, remarking on the improvisatory quality of the Bartók Second Piano Concerto, I characterized the particularity of the solo agent in this work as spontaneity. Doubtless Liszt was Bartók's model in this. Nevertheless all of Bartók's concertos hew unadventurously to the traditional three-movement form, with individual movements mostly in ritornello form, sonata form, variations, rondo, and the rest. Only the Szymanowsky violin concertos, in the early twentieth century, behaved as freely as Liszt—more freely, in fact, because the thematic recurrences are veiled rather than trumpeted out, as is the case with Liszt. And three-movement form remains popular with Philip Glass, John Adams, Aaron Jay Kernis, Richard Danielpour, and lots of other contemporary composers.

⁕ The Liszt concertos are a hard sell, I know. Let me in conclusion, then, pull out all the stops and brazenly co-opt the competition. My reading of these works as improvisatory is nothing new. The author of the article **concerto** in the old *Encyclopaedia Britannica*—the same man who called the cadenza of the Classical concerto "the appendicitis of concerto form"—brushed off the manifestly important entries by Liszt as mere "fantasias." Tovey loathed Liszt as "the worst influence that ever came into any art since the decline of the Roman Empire."[11] Later he published over 250 "essays in musical analysis" in six volumes without including a single Liszt composition.

Fantasias: why of course. The word "fantasia" denotes an improvisation, or a piece of music written in improvisatory style. There is no more reason to dismiss the Liszt concertos than to rule out Bach's Fantasy and Fugue in G minor, or the Fancy in My Ladye Nevell's

Booke inscribed by William Byrd to the mysterious lady herself, or the Vaughan-Williams Fantasia on a Theme by Thomas Tallis. Liszt, legendary as a piano virtuoso, was also a virtuoso composer, in one of the senses I give to the term, spontaneity being a principal aspect or component of a musician's virtù.

Diffusion: Concerto Textures 5

The concerto is predicated on a duality, the duality of concerto agents; but the distinction between them is not always clearly sustained. So far, in our discussion, clarity in this matter has been taken as a donnée, whether in reference to reciprocity between the two agents, characteristic of the Classical era, or polarity, characteristic of the Baroque. Yet almost from the beginning of concerto history, composers have also wanted to problematize and play with the distinction, conceal it or blur it. My general term for this process, in its several manifestations, is *diffusion*. Like polarity and reciprocity, diffusion can be viewed as another mode of concerto duality—which may seem like a paradoxical proposition, since what is involved is a whittling away of duality into textures that amount to complex unities. Let us see what kind of case can be made for this paradox.

***

I start with technology, at a nodal point in the history of the concerto: the meteoric development of musical instruments in the first half of the nineteenth century. Virtually every instrument partook of this development: strings, keyboard, woodwind, and brass. Stradivarius himself escaped the ash-can of history only because string instruments could be fitted with new fingerboards, bridges, and strings, and played with new-style bows. The metamorphosis of the early piano was more sweeping yet. The fragile fortepiano of Mozart's time had developed far enough even in Beethoven's middle years so that he could recruit it, in the "Emperor" Concerto, for his forceful heroic vision. By the time Messrs. Steinway & Sons were through with the instrument in the 1860s, next thing you know you've got the Van Cliburn Competition. Among other exploits, the piano displaced the violin as the concerto's main protagonist.

The divergence of the piano concerto from other concertos probably deserves more attention than it is going to get in these concerto conversations. I do, however, want to draw attention to a sense in which the piano's growing presence eroded the distinction between solo and orchestra. This may seem like another paradox—for does not the piano stand aside with its own sound-world, separate from the orchestra, and do not the violin and the cello, as themselves constituents of the orchestra, share sonorities with it? But as I have already pointed out, one aspect of the piano's virtù is mimesis of an orchestra. It is a far from negligible aspect: the great symphonic repertory of the nineteenth century was known to the public less from concerts than from piano arrangements, arrangements for piano four-hands. The piano can simulate an orchestra; anything the orchestra can do a piano can do, if not better, at least plausibly and often with panache. There is a rough parity between orchestra and piano as there is not between orchestra and violin, or orchestra and cello.

This parity was already an invitation to diffusion: an invitation that Liszt accepted in a topsy-turvy way when he wrote his *Concerto pathétique* for two pianos (and no orchestra) in 1877. Though this may not be a very persuasive piece *qua* concerto, Liszt was as usual asking the visionary questions—never more so than in his late years. And if the solo member of the concerto duality was destined to become more orchestral, certainly the orchestral member was destined to grow more soloistic. For Vivaldi and Bach, with some exceptions, including the Brandenburg Concertos, which is no mean exception, and we shall return to it later—for Vivaldi and Bach, the orchestra consisted of no more than strings and continuo. The Bach sons and the young Mozart added pairs of horns and/or oboes, sometimes as optional accessories, and later Mozart expanded his orchestra to include the multicolored Viennese *Harmonie,* or woodwind group. He never allowed extended solos for its individual members, however. This step seems to have been taken by Beethoven, in his First Piano Concerto of 1795, with its prominent clarinet solo in the slow movement.

With this development, the singularity of the soloist came increasingly into question. Another route began opening up to diffusion. After the Classical era of the symphony, in the decades around 1800, the orchestra steadily expanded, diversified itself, and articulated itself in increasingly unpredictable ways. The symphony encroached upon the concerto—or simply ingested it, as in the second symphony by Berlioz, *Harold in Italy;* commissioned as a viola concerto for Paganini, its disinclination to be that carries symbolic resonance for the present discussion. Later, even a classicizing symphony such as the Brahms First could admit a substantial solo violin part. For a concerto soloist, the late nineteenth-century orchestra spelled potential trouble.

One doesn't have to think very long about Mahler's orchestration to understand why Mahler never wrote a concerto. Karol Szymanowski did, and the orchestra in his two violin concertos is about the richest to be found in the concerto repertory. The orchestral particularity here is color rather than mass or power or discourse—kaleidoscopic color. The problem with these unquestionably distinguished works is not that you can't hear the violin; you always can; but the orchestra is always so much more *interesting*.

، ، ،

One response to this situation from composers was to accept the inevitable and capitalize on the new orchestral resources, by elevating individual instruments to the position of secondary soloists. Generally this happens in a single movement (usually a slow movement) or a longish episode within a movement. The Schumann Piano Concerto must afford one of the first examples, with its clarinet emerging and engaging the solo piano in a long sleepy dialogue that occupies the entire Andante espressivo section of the first movement. In his Cello Concerto, Schumann actually singles out the orchestral cello part as an obbligato line, posing the question of solo singularity in the most acute form. Obviously he wanted the sense of diffusion caused by this doubling, though composers have often gone out of their way to make it impossible. It's a rare clarinet concerto that includes clarinets in its orchestra, and the Violin Concerto by Roger Sessions, for one, uses an orchestra without violins. Sessions knew the Berg Violin Concerto, and Berg employs the orchestral violins quite sparingly and sometimes as a means of diffusion, as we shall see in a moment.

Examples of prominent secondary soloists abound in the standard concerto repertory—the Brahms Second Piano Concerto with its cello, Carl Nielsen's Flute Concerto with its trombone, the Shostakovich First Piano Concerto with its trumpet and his First Cello Concerto with its French horn. Dvořák's Cello Concerto has its flute, a curious case because rather than staying with a particular episode or movement the flute keeps turning up when least expected, like one of those small birds on the back of a hippopotamus. And it is hard to refrain from mentioning the Second Piano Concerto by Chaikovsky, in the huge slow movement of which the piano appears to withdraw as solo instrument in favor of a solo violin-cello pair that suddenly materializes out of the orchestra; after a long while, though, the piano returns and the solo strings fall silent; and then after another long while they come back in again and play cadenzas, among many other things, before leaving the field (and the finale) to the piano.

Looked at differently, secondary soloists can be seen as a protectionist strategy on behalf of the solo. The solo co-opts other instruments by extracting them temporarily from the orchestral mass. Secondary soloists can take some of the load off the soloist in its negotiations with the orchestra; they mediate between solo and orchestra, as Elliott Carter has put it. His Piano Concerto, written in 1966, makes continual use of a subsidiary group of three woodwinds and four strings that Carter calls the concertino. Later Carter concertos do something similar.

Nielsen's procedure is simpler but also somewhat similar in his Flute Concerto, dating from 1931. No doubt protectionism was well advised with so frail a solo instrument, and the piece makes almost systematic use of duets and trios between solo and secondary soloists. The flute seeks out partners promiscuously; as well as the unrefined trombone in the first and third movements, there is a faithful clarinet in the first movement and a casual bassoon in the second. The clarinet supports the flute right away during the first theme, helps out in the cadenzas, and steps in when the flute can't go low enough to make a rather overheated transition.   Example 29

Especially striking is the use of secondary soloists in another work of around the same time, the Violin Concerto of Stravinsky. Here the strategy was not protectionist nor in the least lighthearted. Stravinsky had a clear aesthetic agenda, which had already affected his first concerto, the Concerto for Piano and Wind Instruments. He was of course not the first composer to react against the dramatics of the Romantic concerto. Debussy, in a letter of 1909 to Edgard Varèse, mentioned vaguely some new ideas he had about the genre, which would militate against what he called the "rather ridiculous battle between two characters."[1] (Debussy had soured on the concerto after withdrawing a student effort, the *Fantaisie* for Piano and Orchestra of 1890. The music has been recovered and deserves more exposure.) Ravel expressed himself similarly. Stravinsky would ultimately tell Robert Craft that in this project "the violin in combination was my real interest"—hardly a remark one can imagine coming from Vivaldi or Paganini, nor for that matter from Szymanowski or Prokofiev.[2]

Next Stravinsky praised Balanchine, who choreographed the ballet *Balustrade* to this music, for his *pas de deux* complementing the duets that stand out in all of the movements. For although the work requires a large orchestra, this mostly breaks down into small chamber-musical groups with the solo violin, duets being especially prominent in the finale. Stravinsky also noted casually that a two-violin duet in the finale might bring to mind the Concerto for Two Violins by Bach.

This is diffusion in an advanced form, and another such example is furnished by another product of the concerto-rich 1930s, the Violin Concerto by Alban Berg. In the so-called *Weheklage* section at the end of this work, at the same time as the orchestra works its way through variations on the Bach chorale the solo violin traces surging chromatic lines of lament. And after being told to put on the mute, the solo violin must also suffer first one, then two, then more orchestral violins to join it and double its melodic line. An annotation in the score insists that this *Kollektiv* (Berg's term) be both heard and seen, witnessed, born witness to, by the audience. An entire community must be perceived as joining in lament.

Diffusion: composers achieve this in various ways. Berg denatures or blanches out the solo presence by means of muting and doubling. Nielsen and Stravinsky undermine solo singularity by matching up the solo with proliferating secondary soloists in duets and the like. And Stravinsky also does something else. The third movement of his Violin Concerto, which is entitled Aria II, ends with the violin merging with the orchestra—here reduced to flutes and cellos and basses playing harmonics—to form a single texture. The solo instrument (marked *flautando!*) can almost no longer be heard, only the novel composite texture. It depends on the performance, obviously, or the recording.

Example 30

Diffusion in this case entails coalescence, rather than denaturing or proliferation. We have come across this phenomenon in the same composer's Concerto for Piano and Winds, at the great climax of the first movement (see Example 9). The wind-instrument dirge is overlaid by the piano pulse, both of them magnified unimaginably, a texture exhilarating in its sheer plenitude and intricacy. At the other end of the dynamic spectrum, Bartók does something analogous in both his Second and Third Piano Concertos, in the central, fast "trio" sections of the two slow movements. The piano temporarily steps back as a solo instrument and takes its place in an ad hoc night-music orchestra, a characteristic Bartók combo of special-effect strings, muted brass, piano, xylophone, and sputtering high woodwinds. Like Stravinsky, Bartók creates fascinating textures specific to these works, of course, and in another sense specific to the genre concerto.

◦◦◦◦◦◦

It is late in the day to be bringing up concerto textures. Musicologists are slow to discuss musical texture because this is notoriously hard to do, and the results are usually unhappy. Of all music's parameters the most resistant to theory and verbal description is sonority, whether the sonority of single sounds, timbre, or that of multiple combined sounds, texture. Stanley Cavell once noted that "music has, among the arts, the most, perhaps the only, systematic and precise vocabulary for the description and analysis of its objects,"[3] and then he went on to comment trenchantly on the effect this has had on music criticism; however, Cavell must have had in mind, as most critics at that time did, pitch, harmony, and rhythm rather than texture. As far as the description of texture is concerned, music's vocabulary leaves very much to be desired.

So in brief: analysis of concerto textures works well enough when the solo is accompanied by the orchestra, falters when the relationship between them is contrapuntal, and all but collapses when the solo appears to be accompanying the orchestra. One cannot theorize, one can only admire.

Accompaniment texture, in fact, I did touch on briefly before; it was when the matter of relationships came up, relationships between the two concerto agents. These I categorized as either vertical or horizonal, immanent or dynamic. My discussion of the Chaikovsky Violin Concerto began with a clear, immanent MISTRESS/SERVANT relationship; when the violin sings her song the orchestral instruments regress into a big guitar, and when she turns to bravura, however loudly they play they never intrude. In the second movement, the primary role seems less that of MISTRESS than DREAMER or SEER or MEDIUM. Rather than engaging in display or theatrics, the solo falls into a trance of some sort, and the accompaniment role becomes that of DEVOTEE or COMMUNICANT. Absorbed, abstracted, the solo does not hear the orchestra, whose accompaniment is very quiet, almost breathless; only after some significant action does the orchestra gain profile. The relationship story Chaikovsky tells ends with less simple textures in the finale, where richer roles for the concerto agents spell new mutual awareness.

At the risk of underscoring the obvious, accompaniment textures can be thought of according to the figure-ground model—the solo as figure, the orchestra as ground. But the model will not necessarily invert. A solo instrument resists serving as a ground for an orchestra. When the orchestra material is primary and the solo secondary, however neutral and banal that secondary material may appear, it still projects the authority of its instrumental virtù. Some of the most characteristic and fascinating of concerto textures arise in these situations.

They can arise even with solo subsidiary material of the most elementary kind—such as a stationary pedal note. Recall Mendelssohn's brilliant gloss, in his Violin Concerto, on the Beethoven Violin Concerto. In both composers' opening movements, the exposition of the second theme begins in the woodwinds, Beethoven's violin meanwhile holding on to a superior pedal, a long trilled E above the staff. The first outing of the second theme in the new key, the dominant key—surely that counts as a major phase in the musical discourse. Yet a bravura element, the violin's first trill, is also on display and refuses to register as mere accompaniment. Mendelssohn gives *his* violin nothing but a low, open-string G, marked *pp:* instead of bravura, the very lowest common denominator of violinistic virtù. Even here, as he knew, the solo will refuse to be grounded. (Mendelssohn uses a long plunge to highlight his low G, too: an uncharacteristically brazen move. Later Prokofiev, in a gesture of defiant humility, would gloss Mendelssohn by starting his Violin Concerto No. 2 with open-string G played by the solo mezzo piano, the orchestra silent.)

Example 31

It cannot be said that the figure/ground model will *never* invert. But one is well advised to look sharply at composers who allow this to happen very often. A passage near the start of Schumann's Piano Concerto—the first passage where the piano and orchestra play together after the woodwinds and piano have separately played the first theme—will bring up, not for the first time, Schumann's reputed weakness in orchestration (see Example 13, bars 24–25). The piano arpeggios do indeed sound merely accompanimental, merely dull; in the instrument's middle range they lack the character they need to be perceived as a distinctive texture. Yet this muddy sound forms a matrix from which a new, somewhat vigorous motivic idea can emerge, develop, and finally shake free. The whole passage is perfectly well conceived in terms of texture as well as in draftsmanship.

Liszt's Piano Concerto No. 2 begins with a chromatic melody in the woodwind choir, the clarinet already languorous in the low middle register. After several fast movements the melody comes back and comes into its own, as concerto regresses to chamber music—a fragrant solo cello with piano arpeggios. The latter can only be counted as accompaniment in an ironic sense, I think; Liszt is playing a special role here, the role of rehearsal accompanist. It's only after we have heard him dash off a little inspirational cadenza that we are invited to admire the virtuoso as HACK. And how reluctant he is to allow the cello a second phrase.

Example 32

On the other hand, a celebrated moment a little later is something else again. Example 33 shows Liszt creating a fused texture, comparable to the Stravinsky passages shown in Examples 9 and 30. The primary material, the chromatic kernel of the original melody, isolated and attenuated, appears high in two solo violins and the flutes; the lower strings play barely audible pizzicatos, and the piano plays simple arpeggiated chords, basically of the same kind as in the previous example. To call this a piano accompaniment would be to underestimate it dangerously, and certainly no one would call it counterpoint. It cannot be categorized, it cannot be analyzed out; it becomes an integral component of the sensuous, indeed erotic, total sonority.

Example 33

Next time around the solo cello returns to join the mix and swoon on behalf of you, the listener—swoon twice. If this music brings to mind *Tristan und Isolde,* know that it predates *Tristan* by many years, both as to time of composition and first performance.

. . .

Choice concerto textures occur at a certain predictable juncture within slow movements of a familiar type, lyric movements in a simple, sometimes very simple A B A form. Mozart called such movements "Romanze." Beethoven was perhaps the first composer to capitalize on the return of A (the second A after B) to create a special texture in which the listener can luxuriate at leisure: this occurs in the Adagio un poco mosso of the "Emperor" Concerto. Berlioz cited the passage in his treatise on orchestration. Every musician, he said, must admire

> the wonderful effect . . . produced by the piano's lingering beat, with both hands in the upper register, while the flute, clarinet and bassoon play the melody over eighth-notes played by the strings in an off-rhythm. In such a combination, the sonority of the piano could not be more enchanting, full of the calm of innocence—the very image of grace.[4]

Example 34

It's not the *fraîcheur* or the *grâce* that I admire, it's the diffusion of the piano sound into an inclusive sonority. The melody, the piano figuration, and the string chords *en contretemps:* all become inseparable constituents of a single concerto texture.

Continuing in this tradition, probably consciously, are piano concertos by Mendelssohn and Chopin; while their piano figurations are more refined than Beethoven's, their melodies are orchestrated with less individuality. Not so in the Ravel Concerto in G, a showcase for virtuoso sound-effects of all kinds—solo, orchestral, and combined. The piano melody in the slow movement (A) returns as a sultry English horn solo, while piano scales and slow trills sleepwalk their way through the upper register. A plain left-hand accompaniment in continuous eighth

Plate 5. Leonard Bernstein in Israel, 1948

notes that has in fact been going non-stop from the beginning of the movement contributes a frame of nostalgia for this exquisite sound-mix. A distant descendant of the "Emperor," this music has put any thoughts of innocence or grace far behind it.

Concertos for strings with movements of this type include Cello Concerto No. 2 by Saint-Saëns, the Sibelius Violin Concerto, Violin Concerto No. 1 by Prokofiev, and the Viola Concerto of William Walton. The Prokofiev is as impressive as the Ravel in the matter of textures, and twice as prodigal, inasmuch as Prokofiev builds his form around two different returns of an opening melody. In the first return of this melody (at the end of the first movement), figuration by the muted violin almost loses itself in a new shimmer of string tremolos, flute, and harp [7:45]. In the second return (at the end of the last movement), the melody in the orchestral high strings is doubled an octave higher by *dolcissimo* trills in the violin. Figuration is now deployed in the woodwinds.

Track 9

Track 10

Were the orchestral violins supporting the solo here, or was the solo bodying out the violins? What is the last sound that was heard—orchestra or solo? Like Tristan and Isolde puzzling out the meaning of "mine" and "yours," the entranced listener is past such questions. The agents have become diffused into a single radiant essence. Duality has been lost in a drawn-out moment of glittering delicacy.

꙳ ꙳ ꙳

Earlier I floated the idea that diffusion can be thought of as one of the modes of concerto duality, along with polarity, the mode characteristic of the early eighteenth century, and reciprocity, characteristic of the Classical and Romantic eras. Can one say that diffusion becomes the characteristic mode, or principle, of the twentieth-century concerto? Reciprocity, it is true—the art of conversation and relationship—seems to have interested fewer and fewer composers over time; but it is doubtful that any single principle could be formulated as reciprocity's successor. Concertos have been altogether too diverse. More than with any other genre, probably, composers have felt free to play fast and loose with the implications, expectations, and values conveyed by the term *concerto*. A strange beast, Anthony Pople calls the twentieth-century concerto, whose generic assumptions, he says, "are as much toyed with as fulfilled."[5]

Still, many have noted that diffusion was certainly one route traveled by the twentieth-century concerto—traveled to the vanishing point. For with complete diffusion, obviously, duality vanishes, and that is what happened in the twentieth-century concerto for orchestra. Made famous by Béla Bartók, this genre also includes less well-known exemplars by Hindemith, Kodály, Lutosławski, and quite a few Americans—Walter Piston, Roger Sessions, Elliott Carter, and Gunther Schuller, among others. To be sure, composers define the concerto for orchestra very liberally. Sometimes they seem to mean by it no more than a multimovement work for orchestra that prefers not to be appraised by the standards of the symphony, whatever they may be, while still asking to be taken more seriously than a suite or a sinfonietta. Of those I have been able to hear, the one that feels most like a concerto for a good number of the orchestra members, without any of them standing out as principal, is the Concerto for Orchestra by Zoltán Kodály, composed in 1940. Bartók knew the Kodály when he composed his own Concerto for Orchestra only a few war years later.

The later concertos of Stravinsky are also in effect concertos for orchestra, among them the "Dumbarton Oaks" Concerto of 1938 for small orchestra and *Ebony Concerto* of 1945 for Woody Herman's swing band. Stravinsky reminds us that that is what a big-band jazz number *is*—a four-minute concerto for orchestra, jazz orchestra. His concerto output marks progressive stages of his Neoclassical project: from the

Concerto for Piano and Winds, with its neo-Baroque polarity, to the Violin Concerto, which comes as close to a diffused concerto as we are likely to hear under that title, to "Dumbarton Oaks." Stravinsky evoked the Bach Two-Violin Concerto in connection with his own Violin Concerto, and the Brandenburg Concertos serve ostentatiously as models for "Dumbarton Oaks."

This winds back the clock, and brings us to the final topic of this lecture. Although we began with modern technology, with the extraordinary development of musical instruments in the first half of the nineteenth century, it must not be thought that imaginative concerto textures waited for these developments. The birds in Spring, and the chattering of teeth in Winter: these are perhaps the most striking of the special textures in "The Four Seasons," a work that stands out as much for the variety of its textures as for its mimetic profusion. Nor, of course, is this an isolated case in Vivaldi's immense oeuvre. His first published concertos, the widely influential *Estro armonico* of around 1711, include several for four violins, a solo group chosen specially to provide unusual textures.

One of these concertos for four violins goes further in this regard than the others; and sure enough, that is the one that was transcribed for four harpsichords by J. S. Bach. Presumably Bach was interested to see what new textures could be obtained by transforming Vivaldi's. One does not need to hear many Bach cantatas to appreciate his interest in novel textures. His interest in concerto textures in particular is shown most graphically by the set of six concerti grossi he brought together to present to the Margrave of Brandenburg. As everyone knows, each has a different solo group and a different orchestra. Each creates its own sound world.

The Brandenburg Concertos include some episodes of pure texture music, no doubt inspired by Vivaldi. In the tuneless wash of sonority that surfaces in the middle of the first movement of Brandenburg Concerto No. 5, the three solo instruments, flute, violin, and harpsichord, diffuse away; later a secondary solo cello materializes to enrich a new diffused texture. It's well known that Bach was writing his and the world's first harpsichord concerto with this work, a feat that seems to have involved him in a systematic exploration of the possibilities of the instrument for its new role. He tries it out in many ways: as a member of a quartet with violin, flute, and continuo (in the first movement); as a melody instrument set concerto-fashion against a very lightly scored ritornello (in the second); as a voice in a fugue (in the third); and as a virtuoso instrument playing high-speed runs overlaid on trio action as preface to a spectacular written-out cadenza. In the episode illustrated in Example 35 he tries out the harpsichord in an even more interesting role, as an ingredient for a composite concerto texture.

Example 35

Each Brandenburg has its own sound world, and only one of them would have been familiar to the Margrave and his Kapell. Brandenburg Concerto No. 3 is scored for a plain string band, without any of the gambas, flutes, trumpets, concertante harpsichords, and the like shown off by its companions. Yet the first movement of Brandenburg No. 3 may be the most subtle of them all in terms of texture. In a concerto grosso, after the full orchestra plays the ritornello, individual instruments split off as various different solos or solo combinations. This process is simply another kind of diffusion, diffusion of orchestral corporeality—the inverse, as it were, of diffusion of solo singularity. In Brandenburg No. 3 the process is carried out with the greatest of imagination, as though Bach took the very plainness of his chosen resources as a challenge. If Brandenburg No. 5 can be viewed as a dissertation on keyboard sonorities, No. 3 is a veritable anthology of string sonorities, some well known and others invented by Bach for the occasion.

To mention just a few of these textures: even the seemingly innocent ritornello that starts the piece manipulates texture in a way that no other Bach concerto ritornello seems to do. Opening in three-part harmony, this soon coalesces into two parts and finally into octaves, thus attaining a climax of resonance [0:14]. After the ritornello's cadence in bare octaves, the orchestra crumbles into close-harmony bunches of three solo violins, three violas, and three cellos, moving down the octaves. This becomes a textural matrix for many other episodes that follow. Thus a powerful episode toward the end of the movement—powerful harmonically and because of a new rhythm—substitutes spread violin-viola and violin-cello pairs, moving down the octaves, for the three-instrument bunches [3:27, 4:14].

Track 11

The second time the entire ritornello is heard, only 30 bars after the first time, the music is up an octave and seems to be reorchestrated as a solo for a rapidly shifting number of instruments. A shifting solo, or is it really half-orchestral? Fluidity replaces duality; the orchestra/solo distinction no longer holds. The effect is kaleidoscopic, and for those who accurately remember the original ritornello, almost vertiginous. Where before there were octaves there is now harmony, and where before there was harmony there are now bare octaves, or a three-violin bunch with a viola bunch in the background [1:22].

The one moment in this piece that has evinced the most comment (unless that be a missing moment, the missing slow movement) is the beginning of the third large section of the first movement, the point where the original ritornello theme may be expected to return in the tonic key. It does, with this difference: the ritornello theme is played not orchestrally but by a solo violin, combining, quite exceptionally, with a new solo theme in another violin [2:46].[6] The new, more deliberate theme receives a (real) fugal answer; a triple fugue could be beginning, making use of a new bass in triple counterpoint. Ironically, what is most innovative about this place thematically is most traditional texturally, for Bach now deploys the standard Baroque trio with two violins over a continuo, winding around themselves and merging into thirds and sixths.

And then this homely texture opens up into a great sunburst of sound [3:07]. If the octaves at the end of the original ritornello mark the point of maximum resonance, this massive, pulsating sound stands at the other pole, as the point of maximum sonorous intricacy. To clinch the effect of this ten-voiced texture—an effect of truly Baroque extravagance; Vivaldi would have recognized it with an envious shiver—Bach summons up the concerto's most visionary harmonies.

There are many more one-of-a-kind textures in this movement. Surely the listener does not identify, or learn to identify, each as a discrete entity—a tough assignment even if crystal-clear performances of this music could be taken for granted (and they cannot be so taken). The more he or she responds to the continual flux of texture, however, to the textural iridescence that comes about as the polymorphous orchestra fragments and coalesces, the better.

As it happens, three books on Bach's concertos have appeared in recent years, by English and American scholars alone, and I naturally looked to see what they have to say about Brandenburg Concerto No. 3.[7] They say little, and less that is new, but after all this does not surprise, for as is typical in musicological studies, the authors are concerned with many things but not with texture. Michael Marissen is interested in the Brandenburg Concertos' religious symbolism. Malcolm Boyd is interesting on the prehistory of Brandenburg No. 1. Laurence Dreyfus has illuminating things to say about form and discourse, what he calls "invention," in about a dozen Bach concerto movements or concerto-like movements. Brandenburg No. 3 is not among them. For while there is much to admire in it from this standpoint—the new theme in the third section, to look no further—the chief joy of this music is sensuous, not discursive. Of course Bach's sensuousness is not Liszt's or Ravel's; it is more intellectual and less come-hither. Nevertheless, listening to Brandenburg No. 3, I do not trace the form and still less do I track the textures; I lose myself in their multiplicity and unexpectedness and efflorescence.

The Sense of an Ending 6

The Charles Eliot Norton Professor of Poetry twenty years ago was Frank Kermode, and I must thank him for supplying me (I am afraid he had no choice) with the title of this final concerto conversation.

I am not entirely easy about this appropriation. "The sense of an ending" is exactly what I want to talk about, but it is not possible on this occasion to do any kind of justice to Kermode's fine book, which has become a classic since it first appeared in 1967. Kermode discovers the model for literary fictions in eschatological history—paradigmatically in the Bible, which begins with Creation and ends with Apocalypse. (Like *The Ring of the Nibelung*.) Man in the middest, says Kermode—the phrase is from Sidney's *Apology for Poetry*, a favorite text of mine: man in the middest needs such models as solace, to make tolerable his own moment between beginning and end.[1] The book is subtitled "Studies in the Theory of Fiction," and literary genres such as the novel, tragedy, and autobiography are seen as answering a need to "speak humanly of life's relation to [time]—a need in the moment of existence to belong, to be related to a beginning and to an end." For Kermode, fictions are resolutely temporal and linear; time is always vividly present in his discourse, and therefore his book resonates at once for musicians, who of all artists deal with articulations of time the most abstractly and, it is usually thought, the most subtly.

When Kermode speaks of "one's need to know the shape of life in relation to the perspectives of time," he could almost be defining music, in fact. Inasmuch as duration can be perceived only when it is organized, such organization humanizes time, in Kermode's phrase, by giving it form, and he takes note of the imaginative investments we make in coherent patterns to provide a consonance between beginning, middle, and end. Much else in his theory of fiction is suggestive to musicians. I mention one point for future reference, his interpretation of the perepeteia in classical tragedy and other fictions. Just as it is characteristic of apocalyptic prophecies to be met with what Kermode calls "clerkly skepticism"—for while the hour of Apocalypse is never disproved by learned commentators, it is repeatedly interrogated and revised and delayed—so in literary fictions perepeteia delays closure without ever of course escaping it. Only naive fictions proceed directly to the End; sophisticated listeners or readers demand perepeteia, diversions that with time have grown more and more resourceful and elaborate. Kermode here could almost be talking about musical structures as analyzed by Heinrich Schenker.

◂ ◂ ◂ ◂

What has this to do with the sense of an ending in concertos, however? One common and typical way of ending a concerto, the rondo finale of Mozart, Beethoven, and beyond, has already come up in these conversations. There is nothing apocalyptic about the mutual rondo. It spells accommodation, acceptance, and collusion, which it is easy to associate with high comedy as it flourished in the eighteenth century: Goldsmith and Sheridan, Marivaux and Beaumarchais, Mozart and Da Ponte. Comedy is not about endings, of course. That is the province of tragedy.

Comedies are about beginnings, more or less confident beginnings, about getting along with a life after delays, diversions, setbacks, and general craziness.

There exists, however, one very famous concerto that turns the mutual rondo on its head, with extraordinary results: Mozart's Piano Concerto in D minor, K. 466. It is necessary to address the whole of this piece—that which is ended, as well as the ending—and along with it the hardly less famous Concerto in C minor, K. 491. These works are very much to my present purpose, for in them Mozart found an alternative way of ending. So far from comedy, critics discussing these works evoke tragedy, at least obliquely, and often directly, as we shall see.

Mozart wrote only two concertos in the minor mode, these two, and it's clear that up to a point he modeled the C minor on the D minor, written a year earlier. In both first movements, when the solo enters after the opening orchestral ritornello, it does not do the usual thing and replay the opening orchestral music. The solo enters with a new theme, determined to set its own agenda; long-range replay is replaced by long-range counterplay. Both solo entry themes share some technical characteristics (upward octave leaps, downward scales, the extending sequence, the halting accompaniment in close harmony) and also share a mood—pensive, troubled, and somewhat hesitant (Example 36a and c). And in both concertos, something unusual also happens after the second orchestral ritornello. At this point the unassertive solo themes return to instigate development.

Each development section begins with a modulating dialogue in which solo and orchestra reflect on the entry theme, 26 bars long in the D-minor work and 34 in the C-minor, and then each moves on to a climactic sequence around the circle of fifths prior to the final extended dominant. As always, comparing things that are similar can dramatize their differences and point up their respective individuality. While the

Example 36

D-minor development section certainly has its menacing moments, the C-minor plunges more deeply into exigency.[2] This seems to follow from the fact that the solo has assumed an unusually extended role in the preceding exposition section. The piano begins to tilt the balance between the two concerto agents in its own favor; the piano assumes the role of INSURGENT, crossing a line, presuming too far on an unspoken understanding with the orchestra. The orchestra in its second ritornello positively snarls, and in the development section the orchestra strikes back, at a confrontational crisis where the piano seems swept away again and again by the snarling orchestral motif. In the parallel passage in the D-minor Concerto, the solo remains in charge. In the C-minor Concerto the striking power is the orchestra's.

Example 37

Parenthetically, let me take note of the importance of this passage for the history of the concerto. Beethoven surely took inspiration from it for the great perepeteia or confrontation in the first movement of the "Emperor" Concerto, which also comes at the climax of the development section—however much this may differ from the Mozart in technical details, to say nothing of the outcome. In its turn, the "Emperor" served as model for many popular concertos in the nineteenth century, becoming thereby an authentic source for the conventional wisdom that says concertos have to be about confrontation.

Returning to Mozart and the first movement of the C-minor Concerto: in the remainder of this movement the tension between solo and orchestra does not let up, and the cadenza and the coda leave the listener with a sense of unease and apprehension. The slow movement provides the expected moment of respite. By generous definition, this idyllic interlude in the relative major key, E-flat major, counts as a movement of the "Romanze" type, also used in the D-minor Concerto. Although the present Larghetto does contain an episode in the minor mode, in C minor, the accents of pathos here are elegantly conventionalized. At most, the episode recalls the previous turmoil through a dimly lit scrim.

The finale returns to the minor mode—not, by the way, a foregone conclusion—and eschews the customary mutual rondo form in favor of a set of variations. That is not extraordinary in itself; a good number of finales make use of variation form, including two others by Mozart. What is extraordinary is the character of the variation theme: a tragic march without any of the trappings of an actual funeral march. Think of the "Eroica" Symphony, or the Chopin Funeral March, with their persistent dotted-note figures, muffled drumrolls, and slow harmonic rhythm—and without Mozart's chromaticism, without Mozart's aberrant long empty places (bar 2 et al. in Example 38). The point is that the invariable topoi of the military funeral ritualize tragedy and thus distance it, whereas in Mozart everything has been made internal, personal, and specific to this piece. Once he had the idea of this kind of theme, no doubt it was hard to go wrong—minor-mode variations would prolong the pathos and nuance it, major-mode variations proffered by the orchestra would highlight it by contrast, and an up-tempo coda back in the minor mode could hardly fail to impress.

Example 38

So one might think. In fact Mozart's procedure, especially in the coda with its obsessive Neapolitan sonorities, could never have been predicted. This coda recalls the central crisis of the first movement with an almost macabre effect. The recall of previous music here is something that happens even more extensively in the D-minor Concerto.

⁀ Which we return to now. The earlier work counts as more radical in this respect, for the pensive, troubled music with which the solo makes its entrance in the first movement does more than drive the development section of this movement. It also returns in a transformation to haunt the finale. For the first time, as Charles Rosen has noted, the first and last movements of a concerto are strikingly unified by means of thematic material—a procedure that was much developed later (we saw a spectacular example in Lecture 2, the Bartók Piano Concerto No. 2). No Mozart concerto prior to the D-minor, says Rosen, "exploits so well the latent pathetic nature of the form—the contrast and struggle of one individual voice against many,"[3] and he remarks that the thematic unity answers to "an inward dramatic necessity, the sustaining of a unified tone demanded by the tragic style." "The power of this character is such," he continues, "that it even spills over into the slow movement"—a Romanze, in fact *the* Romanze that inaugurates the whole series of such movements in the Mozart concertos. It differs from all later movements of the same type in that the idyllic, major-mode, almost vapid opening music gives way to an extended paroxysm of minor-mode violence in the middle. The moment of respite is fractured by new portents of tragedy. An extraordinary concept—extraordinary and unthinkable, as Rosen remarks, outside the context of this particular composition.

Then the finale resumes the music and the mood of the first movement. After an orchestral ritornello that we'll return to in a moment, the solo counterplays with an entry theme that is itself a transformation of the first-movement solo entry theme (see Example 36a and b) [0:56]. And in this finale, just as in the opening movement, the piano calls up the same theme to launch the development section (this being a sonata-rondo, with a development section serving as a rondo episode).

Track 12

The entry theme not only launches the development section, it saturates it. When the piano insists on bringing it back a second time, after the launching, in a new key, the orchestra balks and starts to replay it, only to hear the piano mimic its every attempt [3:40]. The orchestra and solo as PITBULLS; as replays multiply, the contestants seem locked together on some kind of relentless roller coaster, a relationship from hell. To me this stands out as the most uncanny moment in this notoriously "daemonic" artwork. (The passage struck Beethoven, too, who imitated it in his Second Piano Concerto, along with other elements from the same source.)

But long before this development section, Mozart has invented an aberrant rondo theme for the piano that will destroy the very concept of the mutual rondo, and with it the consolations and satisfactions of comedy. It is a wild theme, more an explosive gesture than a tune, and it is *not* replayed and hence domesticated by the orchestra, as would happen in a mutual rondo. When the orchestra starts to replay the piano's music, it cannot continue. Instead it collapses or, rather, erupts into a ritornello of almost incoherent rage [0:11].

My reading of this passage as a breakdown diverges from a standard account of the ritornello here "developing" the material of the solo. This is what you will read in Girdlestone, Hutchings, and elsewhere. But *that* reading, besides overlooking the generic code that calls for replay at this point, not development, seems an impoverished response to the actual music—to the orchestra's stacked-up diminished chords, lock-step sequences, and static pulsations that are themeless and entirely non-developmental. By now the orchestra has completely lost touch with the piano and its aberrant rondo theme. The orchestra is hallucinating about tragic tropes from the first movement.

Mozart in this expository passage has provoked a breach of relations between the concerto agents that feels no less unnerving than the great confrontation in the C-minor Concerto development section. And when later the piano plays the wild theme for a second time, the orchestra starts to replay it and fails for a second time [2:46]. A second perepeteia. And when the piano plays the theme for the third and last time, after its cadenza (which the artist should improvise in the most harrowing way possible)—when the piano plays that wild, compressed gesture of a theme for the third time, the theme is compressed even further, compacted, impacted into a challenge [6:18]. The orchestra cannot face this rondo theme, not again, not with its new aggressive spin. How to bring this extraordinary conception to a conclusion?

Mozart's way is with a sunny, major-mode coda. This certainly sounds to me like a deflection [6:26]. Sunny and—what's the word: ribald. Remember Karoline Pichler's story of Mozart's visit to her home, improvising beautifully at the piano, leaping over chairs and tables, meowing like a cat, and turning somersaults; this has got to be the Mozart who wrote this carnivalesque coda. Why isn't the ribald trumpet tag ever played by the solo? Perhaps Amadeus at the piano stuck it in, laughing his famous idiot laugh, in the last two bars.

To try to gauge the tragedy level in these two profound Mozartian essays in the minor mode would be pretty useless, and an exercise hardly imaginable in today's climate of criticism. Like *Don Giovanni*, a composition weirdly anticipated by the D-minor Concerto, the major-mode conclusion here does little to dispel the shadows cast by this work. Such, presumably, was the view of another former incumbent of the Charles Eliot Norton Chair, Leo Schrade, one of the most learned and influential music scholars of my student days. Schrade lectured on "Tragedy in the Art of Music" in 1963, paying due heed to Aristotelian precepts of tragedy, as many of us did at that time, certainly. Yet in addressing operas such as *L'incoronazione di Poppea* and *Don Giovanni* and their ostensibly happy endings, Schrade observed that these endings did not "dull the sharp edges of the weapon which in the course of the drama had done its work of tragic injuries . . . When all is over and the *lieto fine* reached, it is—significantly enough—the poignant music of the forceful scenes that we retain."[4]

In the D-minor Concerto, the music casts tragic shadows on all of the movements—long shadows—and moments of serenity and ribaldry do not efface them. If shadows do not fall on all three movements of the C-minor Concerto, the C-minor coda makes a tragic culmination such as its companion does not attempt. The D-minor Concerto upends the mutual rondo; the C-minor Concerto ignores it; and in doing so both subvert generic expectations more decisively, we could say (since we are talking about closure), than any other imaginable action their composer could have taken. Yet as is well known, the D-minor Concerto was the great survivor among Mozart concertos in the nineteenth century. Cadenzas written for it by Beethoven, Mendelssohn, Brahms, and Clara Schumann, among others, attest to its performance history. The current Schwann Catalogue still lists more entries for K. 466 (just barely) than for any of its siblings.

It is remarkable, in any case, how long we have had to wait for the appearance of another concerto as dark as these two masterworks of the 1780s.

.ᴗ .ᴗ .ᴗ

For the history of concerto endings in the nineteenth century is a story of variations, elegant or otherwise, upon the *lieto fine*. I can sketch this history only very briefly indeed. While Beethoven held to the mutual rondo in all his concertos, the last dating from 1809, other solutions were soon forthcoming. Carl Maria von Weber offered one in his *Konzertstück* of 1821, a small program concerto that was very popular in its time. According to a well-placed leak by the composer, the piano represents a Chatelaine registering sadness and consternation at the absence of her husband in the Holy Land, until he turns up in the form of an orchestral march heard from afar, pianissimo working its way up to fortissimo. Then she rejoices in cascades of bravura sixteenth-notes—but her knight does not rejoice with her. The orchestra never gets to replay the rondo tune (could not, in fact, play such idiomatic piano music). Mutuality in this concerto finale yields to solo *jouissance*.

Other composers, too, abandoned the mutual feature of rondo finales—the young Chopin, for one. Finally Liszt jettisoned the rondo itself, along with almost every other element of Classical form. Liszt established the ecstatic or heroic or triumphant finale, and this was to become the characteristic nineteenth-century solution.

People scoff at these triumphant endings, but one can make the case that for this repertory, they make better sense than the old mutual rondo, with its message of comic resolution, collaboration, fellowship, and accommodation. Now that the virtuoso had became a powerful model for the Romantic hero, the public performance of concertos was no longer a symbolic exercise in social bonding, as I believe it was with Mozart. The concert was the site of heroic visitations by a series of external eminences. The traveling virtuosi of the time arrived with their own music, played for adulatory audiences, and left for the next conquest. Orchestras cobbled together for the occasion served merely as support, if not as another symbolic field of conquest. Schumann as early as the 1830s was complaining about piano virtuosi and their concertos; Schumann particularly resented their "lustige Rondoweise." It was in such circumstances that Liszt first drafted his E-flat Concerto, and other concerto-like works, at a time when, emerging from a long depression, he first heard Paganini, first met the Abbé Lammenais, and resolved to launch his career again in earnest. It must have felt like a heroic decision, and one can surely sense a personal resonance as well as a societal one in the heroic endings of Liszt's two piano concertos.

Sublime and religious accents, too, find their way onto the final pages of not a few nineteenth-century concertos. The Dvořák Cello Concerto introduces an orchestral chorale, an obvious infiltration from the contemporary symphony. A work with a guaranteed place in the record books, the Piano Concerto by Ferruccio Busoni of 1904, emulates an even more exalted model, the choral symphony. A chorus enters singing a mystical text in the last of its five movements; together they take up about an hour and ten minutes. The Grieg Piano Concerto contrives a sort of pastoral apotheosis: a new, calm, slower melody high in the flute turns up as a complete surprise halfway through a conventional mutual rondo with, as is often the case, ethnic overtones. The camera cuts from a peasant dance to a fast-moving aerial shot of sunrise over the fjords. The same music returns fortissimo and orchestrated to the hilt for the concerto's triumphant conclusion. (Garish, rather.)

Example 39

Meanwhile the mutual rondo still survived, a vestige of more innocent times, or what people thought of as more innocent times. Brahms hunkered down to the mutual rondo in all four of his concerto finales, almost as though in defiance of Liszt (the first of the four was composed in the mid-1850s, right around the time the Liszt concertos were premiered). Brahms's strategy for finales was no less retro than his restoration of the opening orchestral ritornello in first movements, which he actually carried out less dogmatically, and which allowed him to launch his concertos with a symphonic grandeur unsurpassed by any other composer. Hence the special disparity that I, at least, sense between what the opening movements promise and what the finales deliver. The overstuffed finale of Brahms's Piano Concerto No. 1 in D minor seems to me to signal an awareness of this difficulty on the part of the composer.

For his Piano Concerto No. 2 in B-flat, fifteen years later, Brahms took the unusual step of inventing a new structure for a multi-movement concerto. Tovey struggled to characterize the finale as follows: "It is, perhaps, not misleading to say here, as so often of Beethoven's finales, something like this: 'We have done our work—let the children play in the world which our work has made safer and happier for them.'"[5] Sounding more than ever like a Brahms wannabe, when Tovey says "our work" he is referring to Brahms's addition of an extra movement to the concerto cycle, a second movement, Allegro, in D minor—"almost tragic," according to Tovey. After this—only after this—comes the serene Andante with its cello solo, back in the tonic key. (Serene, sometimes almost sedative, though not entirely untroubled. Perhaps the global sense of closure is enhanced by the beautiful solo entry recalling—as happens also in the Grieg Piano Concerto—the piano entry of the first movement.) The serious business of tonal equilibrium having been brought to a conclusion, Tovey felt that the children could come out to play in the fourth movement, a sort of carefree appendix.

One final word on mutuality: mutuality of a new kind was employed (and perhaps invented) by Chaikovsky in the finale of his Piano Concerto, and also adopted by Rachmaninoff. An expansive tune that has been played by the orchestra and then replayed by the piano comes back in the coda, sounded forth by both agents simultaneously, in ecstatic unisons and octaves. Simplicity itself—and as upbeat a consummation as anyone could wish. David Schiff has scoffed at the "inevitable climactic moment [in piano concertos] when the lyricism of a big tune is given the full-blown Hollywood-heroic treatment,"[6] but this was before the canonization of Busby Berkeley, and in any case Chaikovsky, at least, had a point to make with this grand coming-together. Since throughout the piece so many of the themes have been systematically confined to one agent or the other, mutuality here does honest work as reconciliation.

·ᴗ ·ᴗ ·ᴗ

When were these upbeat endings finally brought into question? When did composers (or any single composer) tire of the resolute cheeriness of the concerto? When was a significant concerto first written with a quiet ending? In Mozart's time,[7] but after that perhaps not until the years around World War I, with the first violin concertos of Prokofiev and Szymanowski.[8]

In the interwar period, a cluster of concertos emerged that culminate in lamentation, enacted by a solo violin, viola, or cello. The topos is already present in the precocious Viola Concerto by William Walton, of 1929. This piece looks back shamelessly, one has to say, to the Prokofiev First Violin Concerto (Tracks 9–10); but if the idea came from abroad— the idea, that is, of ending a concerto quietly with music from the beginning—the local version of it differs. Where Prokofiev has a song of disembodied rapture, Walton has a lament, though he does not say what the lament is for. Walton also looked back to the finale of the Elgar Cello Concerto, a late composition, dating from 1919 and usually taken as an expression of universal grief following World War I. Though Elgar's final pages are brisk enough, what remains in the listener's ear after they are over is the uneasy opening movement and the tragic slow section inserted into the finale (see Example 16).

Example 40

This English tradition—I think we can call it that—was crossed with a European tradition stemming from Alban Berg's Violin Concerto of 1935. One of the masterpieces of twentieth-century music, for many this work exists almost in a different world from that of its concerto contemporaries. It ends with lament, in the closing elegy for Manon Gropius, the "Angel" of the dedication. Surging chromatic lines in the violin mourn even as the wind instruments offer the equivocal consolation of a Bach chorale. To be sure, the last page of this piece is problematic, like everything else about it—like the program at its various levels of privacy, like the chorale and the Carinthian folksong, like the recourse to virtuosity, like the tonality and the treatment of the twelve-tone row. After the dissonant *Weheklage* of the violins and the even

Example 41

more dissonant final harmonization of the chorale, French horns provide a glimmering of B-flat-major comfort, like the words "The End" scrolling up after a 1930s movie. Viennese wits are said to have dubbed Berg "the Puccini of twelve-tone music"—those who relocated to Los Angeles might well have switched that to Max Steiner.[9]

Paul Hindemith produced half a dozen chamber concertos for various string instrument soloists in the 1920s, and lament comes to the fore in a small concerto-like elegy called *Trauermusik*. It was written for the BBC on the death of King George V of England in 1936. The Bach chorale in the finale of the *Trauermusik*—it is "Ein könig stimmt"—interrupted by grieving solo viola passages is close in concept to the Berg.

Hindemith's *Trauermusik* is directly quoted in a work actually called *Concerto funebre,* a concerto for violin and string orchestra that also follows Hindemith and Berg in making use of chorales.[10] The composer, Karl Amadeus Hartmann, little known in this country, emerged as a major conservative figure in German music after World War II. He is especially admired for his symphonies: the great German symphonic tradition may be said to range from Haydn to Hartmann. In the Nazi years Hartmann withdrew from the musical life of his fatherland, though his music—some of it with anti-Nazi subtexts—was played elsewhere. The *Concerto funebre* was written in 1939 in the wake of Munich, the Anschluss, and the invasion of Poland. Its overarching threnody encloses a sort of battle symphony, with a machine-gun-fire theme replacing the artillery usually represented in earlier such exercises. In the outer movements the violin mostly engages in passionate lamentation, underpinned periodically by fragmentary chorales in the orchestra.

At the beginning the violin itself plays a chorale, a Hussite hymn still remembered in Czechoslovakia, "Kdož jste Boží boyavníci." It's important that audiences catch this reference, just as listening to the Berg they need to know the unsung words of the Bach chorale. Example 42 shows the end of the opening movement, Introduction (Largo)—Largo.

Example 42

Also in 1939, another precocious English composer took his own measure of the Berg Concerto. Once again, the reference in Benjamin Britten's Violin Concerto, Opus 19, was evidently specific, though not specified; Britten was mourning the Spanish Civil War (with "disarming frankness," according to a review at the time by Elliott Carter. Britten had attended the touch-and-go premiere of the Berg Concerto at Barcelona in 1936, when Scherchen had to take over the orchestra from Webern). The keening violin cantilena with which the concerto closes sounds above a passacaglia, rather than a chorale. The same topos of threnody is encountered in the finest of the Shostakovich concertos, the first Violin Concerto, another work with political overtones; written in 1947, it was withheld for a number of years on account of the Stalin crackdown in 1948. The third movement, a passacaglia, opens with minatory French horns over the first thematic statement and closes with the same music recast for a grieving violin. It is a haunting moment, a moment of great solemnity.

Example 43

Shostakovich does not end on this note, instead segueing by way of a cadenza into a short movement called Burlesca as a finale, after the passacaglia. Short and rather unfortunate, I believe—inadequate both to the previous passacaglia and to the beautiful Nocturne movement before that. Yet as in the Elgar Cello Concerto, as in the Mozart D-minor Concerto, and for that matter, as also in the Stravinsky Concerto for Piano and Winds, with its lively trivia and its recurring dirge—in all of these works the affect of the music at the end does not accord with the ultimate impression of the whole. Whatever their final pages may seem to say, none of these twentieth-century concertos can be thought to end with a *lieto fine*. I do not think, then, that the Stravinsky Piano Concerto with its puppet ending celebrates the subhuman, in Richard Taruskin's term. Leo Schrade's words apply in this case too: "When all is over and the *lieto fine* reached, it is the poignant music of the forceful scenes that we retain."

At the risk of underscoring the obvious, let me make two general points about these concertos of lamentation. First, they depend on and exploit a relatively new aspect of violinistic virtù, if I may return to the word I have used to enlarge the concept of instrumental virtuosity. Musical instruments imitate the voice, in song, declamation, outcry, or lament. The keening voice is a woman's voice; the violin models a soprano or a contralto singer. The connection probably clicked in at a certain historic concert in 1829, when a violin joined a woman singing Bach's "Erbarme dich" instead of a boy, but concerto composers seem hardly to have grasped it until this century. For Karl Amadeus Hartmann, lament becomes the particularity of the solo agent for the greater part of his *Concerto funebre*. Hartmann's lament is inconsolable, as it had to be, given its subject.

The second point is that the distinctive topos developed by these composers is specific or intrinsic to the concerto genre. Mourning is universalized by being apportioned between the two concerto agents: personal utterance is given to the soloist, while the orchestra speaks for the community through its chorale or its passacaglia. This apportionment arises naturally from the concerto's special kind of duality; it is not something that could happen in a symphony. Berg paints an even more complex picture, as his orchestra separates out into winds and strings, with the dirge of the wind chorale in counterpoint with an individual song that is gradually diffused and universalized by orchestral violins. (This orchestral division recalls to me, at least, and however oddly, the Chaikovsky Violin Concerto. Chaikovsky's slow movement features ecclesiastical wind sounds and a solo melody that registers, after all, something like a well-manicured lament.)

And one more point: this intensive double projection of mourning goes some way toward validating a somewhat ambitious analogy about the concerto that was drawn in the eighteenth century, the analogy between the concerto agents and the protagonist and chorus of Greek tragedy. A formal element in tragedy that combines chorus with actor is the *kommos*, or dirge. A kommos that is held up as exemplary is in the *Choephori,* in the scene where Electra and Orestes meet at Agamemnon's tomb to mourn him, their stanzas alternating with stanzas given to the chorus of libation bearers.[11] The participants sing in different meters and different stanza forms, coordinated into a total structure. Different meters means different musics, and so one can see a parallel between this ancient "antiphonal song or lyric dialogue" and the conjoined solo cantilena and orchestral chorale in our twentieth-century concertos of lamentation.

The Piano Concerto by Elliott Carter of 1965, like most serious music of its time, is for many or most listeners hard to hear, hard to make sense of. It needs hearing many times (in its recorded form; live performances are only too few). Yet the sense of an ending in this piece is stark and unmistakable. None of the nineteenth-century warhorses known for their confrontational energies pit the concerto agents against each other as brutally as does this complex modernist score. Carter himself has spoken of a "battle" between individual and crowd, a battle that reaches its culmination in a shattering passage near the end where the solo seems to take a terrible beating from the orchestra. The roles assumed by the agents, in a relationship story that ends in tragedy, are VICTIM and BRUTE. The composer has even told what was in his ear when he wrote this music: machine-gun fire in Berlin, at the time when the Berlin Wall was going up.

After the orchestra has done with its victim and has left, the piano is heard continuing, while its associated support system—the so-called concertino of secondary soloists—disintegrates, until the piano plays alone and diminuendo, and then just stops. Carter tells the relationship story as follows:

Example 44

> The piano is born, then the orchestra teaches it what to say. The piano learns. Then it learns the orchestra is wrong. They fight and the piano wins—not triumphally, but with a few weak, sad notes.

And again:

> [The piano] is victorious by being an individual—if there is a victory. Anyway, the orchestra stops before the piano does. Maybe that's a victory. I don't know.[12]

David Schiff, an acute critic and champion of Carter, tells the story a little differently: the piano is an anti-hero in the alien world of modernity, the orchestra an insistent and brutal machine. These agents represent violently irreconcilable principles in "an epic confrontation of life against death," and Schiff hears the solo in the final bars as a SURVIVOR, a token of hope in Carter's tragic landscape.[13]

But it can only be hope against hope. For this ending is in fact a second ending, a second series of "weak, sad notes." In an arresting passage shortly before Example 44, the piano's luxuriant, somewhat frantic arabesque collapses into a single note, the F above middle C, repeated again and again—ten times, twenty times, fifty times. Such archetypical gestures of closure occur seldom in the music of modernism. Bursts of orchestral sound around the repeated F are desperate and terrible; especially unnerving is the rhythm. The victim dies and then refuses to die, dies and is not suffered to die, survives to take new punishment. Coming after this, the second ending (it does not reclaim the pitch F) sounds to me less like a win, as Carter has suggested—some-

Plate 6. Vladimir Horowitz

what doubtfully, it seems—or a hope, as Schiff suggests, than like a second dying.

◦◦◦◦◦◦

The Carter Piano Concerto represents some kind of extreme in the history of this long-lived and diverse genre.

And Carter's concerto is a hard act to follow. I can only end this lecture, and this series of lectures, by means of a rather sharp swerve, one still executed under the spell of the extreme ending that is Apocalypse. Frank Kermode's *The Sense of an Ending* still has something to teach us, I think, about the musical Apocalypse.

The decline of the West—to appropriate another book title—has been the burden of many commentators from many areas of cultural activity for a long time. Deterioration if not extinction has been seen in letters, the arts, the media, morals, civility, civic virtue, and the rest. But it seems to be only in the last ten or fifteen years, in the shadow of the millennium, that the End of classical music has been prophesied and proclaimed routinely. Musical composition is faltering, symphony subscriptions are falling off, classical lines of recordings are failing, music education is lapsing, and holding leisurely conversations about concertos as the millennium approaches will seem to some observers like fiddling—with the *Danse macabre* by that most faithful of nineteenth-century concerto composers, Camille Saint-Saëns, on my music stand—while Rome burns. The Norton Lectures: to what end? And lest we forget, Rome may one day burn in another Apocalypse, or some more precariously located modern megalopolis: the nuclear Apocalypse.

Or the bioweapon Apocalypse. This we need to take more seriously than we seem able to do. The eschatological discourse of classical music, on the other hand, though we need to take it seriously enough, has to face up to the "clerkly skepticism" that Kermode found characteristic of these situations. (Three years ahead of time, Stephen Jay Gould published a little book called *Questioning the Millennium,* really a long essay on Kermode's clerkly skepticism.) It is not clear, to begin with, that the prospect of the End agitates many listeners to classical music. Rumblings come, rather, from the academy and from the press, in the first place from revisionist musicologists impatient with the canon of Western music and its coercive, exclusionary effects. But while I am generally sympathetic to revisionism in my field, this strand of it strikes me as suspect and curiously half-hearted. Edward Said deplores the coerciveness of symphony concerts and then goes home to play arrangements of Brahms chamber music on his piano. Susan McClary sets out to deconstruct Mozart and then manages quite beautifully to inscribe his G-major Piano Concerto, K. 453, more firmly into the canon than ever before.[14] Examples could be multiplied. Evidently music is still needed to console man and woman in the middest.

As for the press: the alarm and the alarums of symphony orchestras and other musical institutions at their graying audiences, greedy music managers, and ungrateful union musicians—this makes good copy, a change of pace after a round of notices devoted to actual music, the music critics' daily work. Always newsworthy, too, are the maneuvers of the big record companies struggling to maintain and maximize profits. The industry recently launched another of its periodic technological fixes, or perepeteias, the DVD disc.

This one may not work. And no doubt more symphony orchestras will fail. That the institution itself will fail, however, is doubtful, in part for a reason that musicologists impressed by Marx and Baudrillard find it so regrettable. The symphony concert remains one of the few arenas left for ritual interchange and display by the wealthy and the powerful, and while this elite has grown and is growing exponentially, it has yet to invent alternative means of self-celebration. Until that happens, I suspect, the symphony concert will survive as an efficacious, ongoing, and relatively painless institution for social bonding. What is more, another significant elite, that of the academy, also requires music for its social formation (as witness, in a small way, this occasion). It will not forgo its chamber music concerts and records and lectures.

Some record companies, too, will fail. Let it not be forgotten, though, that the important thing about music on records is that CDs are played, not that CDs are purchased—consumption, not commodification. The Schwann Catalogue will doubtless shrink considerably, or shrink dramatically, and indeed it's likely that listening in the future will take place from a limitless online digital stockpile.

This strikes many older persons as very chilly, no doubt, to say nothing of music professionals of all ages. Music mechanically reproduced is music without aura, in Walter Benjamin's endlessly cited formula, an egregious casualty of Adorno's "regression of hearing." Well, we are living in *our* world, not the world of Benjamin and Adorno. By now, several generations after the dissemination of sound recording, now a hundred years old, the conditions for music have—changed. This change is comparable, I have argued, to another paradigm shift that happened or began to happen about a thousand years earlier in the history of Western music: the introduction of musical notation, the writing-down of music.[15] Musical notation made possible, as generation followed generation, first organum and conductus, then motet and mass, madrigal and opera, symphony and concerto.

And certainly this was not accomplished without a "regression of hearing." As time went on, musicians found themselves singing from a book, singing by sight, not by ear—singing something unknown to them and alien and transitory. This was disturbingly unlike the interiorizing of melodies that singers had communally learned by heart as choirboys, and summoned up repeatedly, yearly or daily, from a huge repertory of memorized ancient song. More troubling yet, the new music was no longer sung by the entire monastic community of Christendom. It was cultivated by a new literate elite increasingly associated with secular institutions. An incalculable loss of aura, and a calculable gain in musical repertory.

The experience, the consolation of classical music today is attained more and more through recordings, rather than through live performances. This has been happening for some considerable time. The paradigmatic figure in current music is not the unlettered clerical singer of Gregorian chant, nor the piano student sight-reading a new score, nor the affluent symphony subscriber, but the lone aficionado of historic recordings and surround sound. He or she has suffered another incalculable deprivation of aura, with again a calculable gain in repertory. As I think back on my former argument, I would now add that today's solitary listening seems a return to or, rather, an apotheosis of the Romantic ideal of self-consciousness modeled in music, celebrated by figures such as Tieck, E. T. A. Hoffmann, and Schopenhauer—that absorption in music-in-itself, absolute music, that is so regretted by revisionist musicologists, regretted even more than the persistence of the classical-music canon. History produces these ironic regressions.

Music—classical music—will survive under conditions more exiguous than Benjamin and Adorno imagined. Concertos will be heard when they are not played and not seen, or seldom played, or never played—but the artists who once did play them will live on, because of recorded sound. Artur Schnabel, Joseph Szigeti, Jacqueline Du Pré: they already do. Music will survive because it is needed and there is nothing to replace it. As Frank Kermode claimed years ago for literary fictions, in a sentence quoted earlier, music answers to "a need to speak humanly of a life's importance in relation to time, a need in the moment of existence to belong, to be related to a beginning and to an end." I think he is right, and I cannot believe he would not agree that music speaks to this too, as well as fictions.

Emerson has a beautiful statement about music. "So is music an asylum," he wrote in one of his journals, and also more than an asylum. "It takes us out of the actual and whispers to us dim secrets that startle our wonder as to who we are, and for what, whence, and whereto."[16]

Conversation-stopper (After-words)

Writing, says Tristram Shandy, "when properly managed, (as you may be sure I think mine is) is but a different name for conversation." Still, with these Norton Lectures, which were well punctuated by sound recordings, video clips, and a few sessions at the piano, turning them into prose required a good deal of reworking, which I have tried to do in a way that does not too much alter the original tone. A point is made in Lecture 4 about the formula "improvised or improvisatory"; the text of this book is not conversation but (I hope) conversational.

As the text of the lectures was by no means overlong, for the book I have filled out detail at a number of points. The CD recording issued with it also allows for the inclusion of, if not whole concertos, at least whole movements of concertos, as would not have been practical at the lectures themselves.

∙⌐ I am happy to have the opportunity to thank two agencies that supported my work on the concerto in its early stages, in 1986 and 1987: the Christian Gauss Seminars in Criticism at Princeton University, and the Rockefeller Foundation Bellagio Center. Winter or summer, they provide environments for work in progress that are pretty much ideal. And speaking of environments, it is appropriate at this time to acknowledge how much I owe to the University of California at Berkeley for support or nurture, really, throughout my career.

⁓ It did not seem right to edit out the strong disclaimer about theory issued at the start of these lectures (page 1), even though very soon after starting to rework them it hit me that I simply hadn't been able to proceed without, in fact, nailing up a rough scaffold of theory. If and when this is to be dismantled, perhaps some of the boards may be salvaged and put to use by other critics, for the concerto is a topic that deserves more attention. An intelligent book came out while my own project was under way: *Das Konzert: Form und Forum der Virtuosität* by Konrad Küster (Bärenreiter Studienbücher Musik, 6; Cassel: Bärenreiter, 1993).

⁓ Music stops words. Complementing the Norton Lectures in Harvard's Paine Hall was a short Concert of Concertos, on March 8, 1998: Bach's Violin Concerto in D minor, BWV 1052a, played by Daniel Stepner in an original transcription of his own; the Copland Concerto for Clarinet, played by David Schneider; and Karl Amadeus Hoffmann's *Concerto funebre*, played by James Buswell. Members of the Harvard-Radcliffe Orchestra were directed by James Yannatos, to whom I am immensely grateful for his cooperation—no, his abounding enthusiasm—as I am to the Department of Music as a whole for their hospitality and patience throughout the year.

It was a stroke of good fortune that the winner of the Harvard-Radcliffe Orchestra's Concerto Contest in 1997–98, Joseph Lin, auditioned with the Chaikovsky Violin Concerto, one of the few works treated at some length in these lectures. He played it at an HRO concert in Sanders Theater just a few days before the last of them, and Mr. Yannatos was good enough to invite me to present a preconcert talk on that occasion. Then came the music . . .

J. K.
Berkeley, May 1998

Notes

Music Examples

Credits

Index

Music on the CD

Notes

1. Getting Started

1. I follow Richard Taruskin in this transliteration; "Tchaikovsky" throws an unwanted and probably hegemonic Germanic light on the Russian composer, who should match up with Chekhov, Chernobyl, and Chomsky. In German scholarly writings the preferred form is now Čajkovskij.

2. Donald Francis Tovey, *Essays in Musical Analysis*, vol. 3, *Concertos* (Oxford: Oxford University Press, 1937), p. 209.

   I have acknowledged my debt to Tovey's work in general on a number of occasions, and do so again in specific reference to his foundational writings on the concerto, in the present volume of his *Essays in Musical Analysis* and elsewhere. This in spite of some impatient remarks made about him later.

3. *Strunk's Source Readings in Musical History*, rev. ed., ed. Leo Treitler, vol. 5, *The Late Eighteenth Century*, ed. Wye J. Allanbrook (New York: Norton, 1997), p. 66.

4. Charles Rosen, *The Classical Style: Haydn, Mozart, Beethoven*, rev. ed. (New York: Norton, 1997), pp. 214–218.

5. See Leon Platinga, *Beethoven's Concertos: History, Style, Performance* (New York: Norton, 1998), ch. 6.

6. But at one point in the development section the drum has played a version of the motif veiled harmonically and rhythmically; see Wolfgang Osthoff, *Beethoven: Klavierkonzert c-moll*, Meisterwerke der Musik, 2 (Munich: Fink, 1965), p. 12.

2. Particularity and Polarity

1. Frank Kermode, *The Genesis of Secrecy* (Charles Eliot Norton Lectures, 1977–78; Cambridge, Mass.: Harvard University Press, 1979), p. 65.
2. Don Michael Randel, ed., *Harvard Concise Dictionary of Music* (Cambridge, Mass.: Harvard University Press, 1978), p. 113. This incipit has not survived, I see, in the 1999 edition.
3. Thomas Clifton, *Music as Heard: A Study in Applied Phenomenology* (New Haven: Yale University Press, 1983), p. 247.
4. Heinrich Christoph Koch, *Versuch einer Einleitung zur Composition* (Leipzig, 1793), vol. 3, p. 332; cited by Jane R. Stevens in *Mozart's Piano Concertos: Text, Context, Interpretation,* ed. Neal Zaslaw (Ann Arbor: University of Michigan Press, 1996), pp. 222–223.
5. See John Warrack, *Tchaikovsky* (New York: Scribner, 1973), p. 164, and Igor Stravinsky, *Chroniques de ma vie* (Paris: Denoël et Steele, 1935), p. 70.
6. Joseph Kerman, "Mozart's Piano Concertos and Their Audience," in *Write All These Down* (Berkeley and Los Angeles: University of California Press, 1994), pp. 322–334. I draw on this essay a number of times in this book.
7. I derive this figure from Vivaldi's best-known concertos, the hundred-odd works published in his lifetime.
8. See Elwood Derr, "Some Thoughts on the Design of Mozart's Opus 4, the 'Subscription Concertos' (K. 414, 413, and 415)," in Zaslaw, *Mozart's Piano Concertos,* pp. 201–207.
9. Stravinsky's appraisal as reported by Artur Rubinstein, *My Many Years* (New York: Knopf, 1980), p. 283. Rubinstein is not always entirely reliable.
10. With double basses, nearly always doubling low wind instruments or the piano left hand; but see Example 11.
11. Stravinsky, *Chroniques de ma vie,* pp. 70–71.
12. Richard Taruskin's term; see "Stravinsky and the Subhuman" in *Defining Russia Musically* (Princeton: Princeton University Press, 1997), pp. 360–457.
13. Mosco Carner, "Béla Bartók (1881–1945)," in *The Concerto,* ed. Ralph Hill (London: Penguin, 1952), p. 334.

3. Reciprocity, Roles, and Relationships

1. "When in Berlin I would seldom miss Möser's quartet evenings; when it comes to instrumental music, these presentations are the most comprehensi-

ble to me. One hears four rational people converse among themselves [*sich untereinander unterhalten*]—one believes that one is getting something out of their conversation and coming to know the characters of their instruments." *Briefwechsel Goethe Zelter,* selected by Werner Pfister (Zurich and Munich: Athenien, 1987), p. 304.

2. See Plantinga, *Beethoven's Concertos,* p. 353 n. 63, and *Beethoven: Werke,* series III, vol. 3, *Kritischer Bericht,* ed. Hans-Werner Küthen (Munich: Henle, 1996), esp. pp. 10–11, and Halina Goldberg, "Chopin in Warsaw's Salons," paper read at the American Musicological Society National Meeting, 1997. In Warsaw reduced-forces performances of concertos were called "quartet performances." The Mozart concertos are Opus 4 (Artaria, 1785), comprising K. 413, 414, and 415.

3. See, for example, James Hepokoski, *Sibelius: Symphony No. 5* (Cambridge Music Guides; Cambridge: Cambridge University Press, 1993), pp. 5–9. A less pejorative term would be "reformulations."

4. Owen Jander, "Beethoven's 'Orpheus in Hades,'" *19th-Century Music,* 8 (1984–85): 195–212; see also ibid., 19 (1995–96): 31–49 and 286–287.

5. More exactly, composed this movement. He expanded his original one-movement Fantasia (the present concerto's first movement) into a three-movement concerto at her urging.

6. A point I made in *Opera as Drama* [1956], rev. ed. (Berkeley and Los Angeles: University of California Press, 1988), p. 188.

7. See Taruskin, *Defining Russia Musically,* pp. 281–290.

8. See ibid., p. 119.

9. Joseph Kerman, "Representing a Relationship: Notes on a Beethoven Concerto," *Representations,* 39 (1992): 80–101.

10. See "Mozart's Piano Concertos" in *Write All These Down.*

4. Virtuosity/Virtù

1. See *Mozart's Piano Concertos,* ed. Zaslaw, p. 224.

2. A *locus classicus* for a dialogue entry that foretells the entire piece is the Variations Symphoniques for Piano and Orchestra by César Franck.

3. "Staging the Virtuoso: Ritornello Procedure in Mozart, from Aria to Concerto," in *Mozart's Piano Concertos,* ed. Zaslaw, pp. 149–186.

4. Robert Layton, ed., *A Guide to the Concerto* (Oxford: Oxford University Press, 1997), p. 209.

5. The classic case of this kind of mimesis, which can be traced all the way back to Vivaldi, is in Ludwig Spohr's Violin Concerto No. 8 in A minor, called the *Gesangszene.* A more familiar case is Rimsky-Korsakov's *Scheherazade,* featuring a solo violin as RHAPSODE.

6. Chick Corea, with Bobby McFerrin and the St. Paul Chamber Orchestra, *The Mozart Sessions* (Sony SK 62601, rec. 1996); see especially K. 466. Between 1996 and 1999 Robert Levin recorded the five Beethoven piano concertos and some other works with John Eliot Gardiner and the Orchestre Révolutionnaire et Romantique (Deutsche Grammophon Gesellschaft). Since 1995 he has been engaged in a complete recording of the Mozart piano concertos with Christopher Hogwood and the Academy of Ancient Music (Oiseau Lyre).

7. See *Mozart: Neue Ausgabe sämtliche Werke,* series V, vol. 7, *Kritischer Bericht,* ed. Hermann Beck (Cassel: Bärenreiter, 1964), pp. g6–7, g10–14. Ployer was identified as the writer after this publication came out.

8. Donald Francis Tovey, *Essays in Musical Analysis, III: Concertos* (London: Oxford University Press, 1937), p. 86. On Tovey's cadenzas, see idem., "Prefaces to Cadenzas to Classical Concertos," in *The Main Stream of Music and Other Essays* (New York: Oxford University Press, 1949), pp. 315–324.

9. See Otto Erich Deutsch, *Mozart: Die Documente seines Lebens* (Cassel: Bärenreiter, 1961), p. 472.

10. For example, the first theme is presented in thick *forte* chords for the piano which make sense only as original triple stops on the violin. The cadenza was transcribed back for violin by Wolfgang Schneiderhan. It is played by Ruggiero Ricci on Biddulph CD LAW 017, rec. 1994.

11. Donald Francis Tovey, *The Classics of Music,* ed. Michael Tilmouth (Oxford: Oxford University Press, forthcoming; cited in Tilmouth's introduction). Tovey's articles for the 11th and 14th editions of the Britannica, 1911 and 1929, are collected in idem., *Musical Articles from the Encyclopaedia Britannica* (London: Oxford University Press, 1944).

5. Diffusion: Concerto Textures

1. *Debussy: Letters,* ed. François Lesure and Roger Nichols (Cambridge, Mass.: Harvard University Press, 1987), p. 211.

2. See Igor Stravinsky and Robert Craft, *Dialogues and a Diary* (New York: Doubleday, 1963), p. 80.

3. Stanley Cavell, *Must We Mean What We Say?* (New York: Scribner, 1969), p. 186.

4. Hector Berlioz, *Traité d'instrumentation et d'orchestration* (Paris: Lemoine, 1925), pp. 91–95.

5. Anthony Pople, *Berg: Violin Concerto* (Cambridge Music Handbooks; Cambridge: Cambridge University Press, 1991), pp. 7, 3.

6. There are no "new" themes, of course: this one has been traced to the viola part in bar 1.

7. Malcolm Boyd, *Bach: The Brandenburg Concertos* (Cambridge Music Handbooks; Cambridge: Cambridge University Press, 1993); Laurence Dreyfus, *Bach and the Patterns of Invention* (Cambridge, Mass.: Harvard University Press, 1996); Michael Marissen, *The Social and Religious Design of J. S. Bach's Brandenburg Concertos* (Princeton: Princeton University Press, 1995).

6. The Sense of an Ending

1. Frank Kermode, *The Sense of an Ending: Studies in the Theory of Fiction* (Oxford: Oxford University Press, 1967), p. 47.

2. This work is discussed further in my essay "Mozart's Piano Concertos and Their Audience," in *Write All These Down*.

3. Rosen, *The Classical Style,* pp. 233–235.

4. Leo Schrade, *Music in the Art of Tragedy* (Charles Eliot Norton Lectures, 1962–63; Cambridge, Mass.: Harvard University Press, 1964), p. 70.

5. Tovey, *Essays in Musical Analysis,* vol. 3, p. 125.

6. David Schiff, *The Music of Elliott Carter* (London: Eulenberg, 1983), p. 228.

7. Robert Levin pointed out to me five Mozart concertos with quiet endings.

8. "The first performance of Prokofiev's Concerto in the Soviet Union . . . was given . . . by two extraordinary nineteen-year-olds, Nathan Milstein and Vladimir Horowitz, the latter playing the orchestra part on the piano. ('I feel that if you have a great pianist like Horowitz playing with you, you don't need an orchestra!'[!] wrote Milstein in his memoirs, *From Russia to the West.*) Milstein and Horowitz introduced Karol Szymanowski's Concerto No. 1 in the Soviet Union on the same occasion." Michael Steinberg, *The Concerto: A Listener's Guide* (New York: Oxford University Press, 1998), p. 350.

9. As reported by Mosco Carner (who was there): see *Alban Berg: The Man and the Music* (London: Duckworth, 1975), p. iv.

10. The title had been used before, for a not very lugubrious concerto for multiple instruments by Vivaldi, RV 549.

11. See Bernhard Zimmermann, *Greek Tragedy: An Introduction*, trans. Thomas Marier (Baltimore: Johns Hopkins Press, 1991), pp. 47–49.

12. Cited by David Schiff, *The Music of Elliott Carter*, pp. 235 and 237.

13. Notes accompanying the recording of Carter's Piano Concerto by Ursula Oppens with the Cincinnati Symphony Orchestra, conducted by Michael Gielen (New World Records NW 347–2, rec. 1984 and 1985), p. 8.

14. See Edward W. Said, *Musical Elaborations* (The Wellek Library Lectures; New York: Columbia University Press, 1991); Susan McClary, "A Musical Dialectic from the Enlightenment: *Mozart's Piano Concerto in G Major, K. 453*, Movement 2," *Cultural Critique*, 4 (1986): 126–169.

15. See "A Few Canonic Variations," in *Write All These Down*, pp. 33–50.

16. *Journals of Ralph Waldo Emerson, 1820–1872*, ed. Edward Waldo Emerson and Waldo Emerson Forbes, vol. V, 1838–41 (Boston: Houghton Mifflin, 1911), p. 211.

Music Examples

Example 1

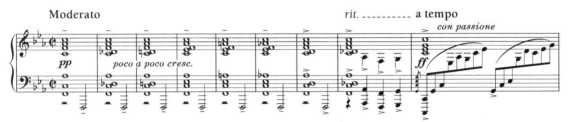

Example 2

Example 3

Example 4

Allegro molto appassionato SOLO
W.W.

Allegretto
STR.
SOLO
TIMP.

Allegro ma non tanto
STR. con sord., CL., BN.
commodo
SOLO
etc.
BN.

Moderato con moto
CYMBAL
TIMP.
pp marc.
mf espr.
mf
SOLO *p dolciss. ed espress.*
HARP, FL.
etc.

Example 5

Example 6

Allegro ma non troppo e molto maestoso

Example 7

a.

b.

Example 8

Example 9

Example 10

Example 11

Example 12

piano continues

Example 13

Allegro affettuoso

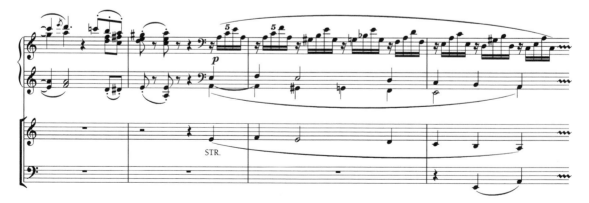

Example 14

Allegro molto moderato

Example 15

Example 16

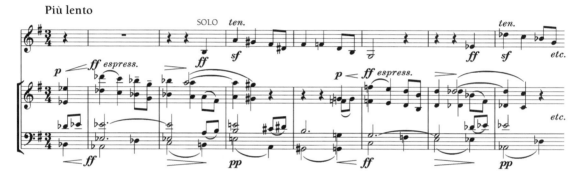

Example 17

a.

b.

Example 18

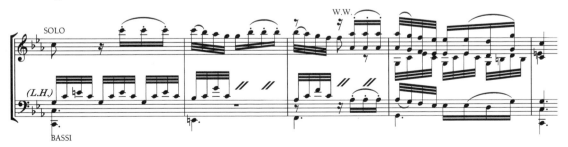

Example 19

Andantino grazioso

Example 20

Example 21

Example 22

a.

b.

c. molto sostenuto il tempo, moderatissimo

Example 23

Example 24

Example 25

Example 26

Example 27

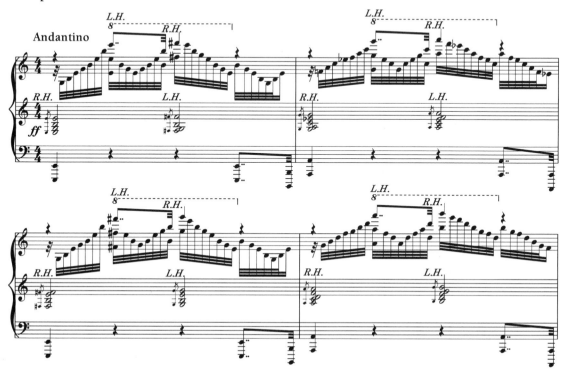

Example 28

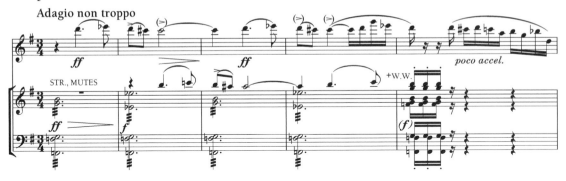

Example 29

Example 30

Example 31

Example 32

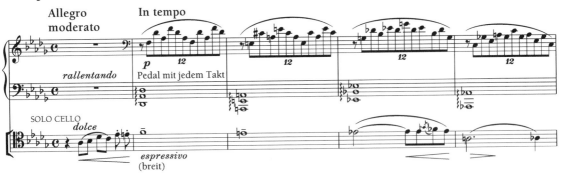

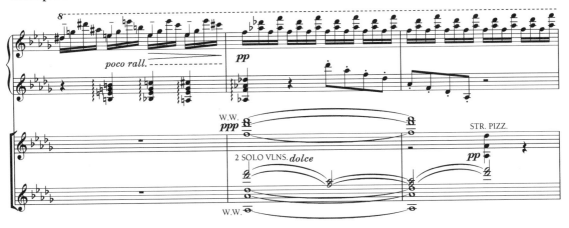

Example 33

Example 34

Example 35

Example 36

a.

b.

Allegro assai

c.

Allegro

Example 37

Allegro

Example 38

Example 39

Example 40

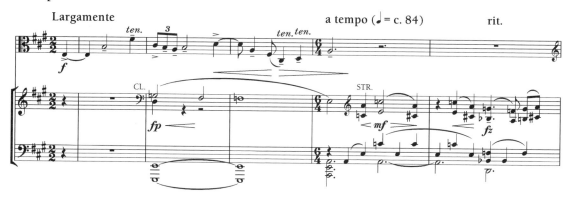

meno mosso

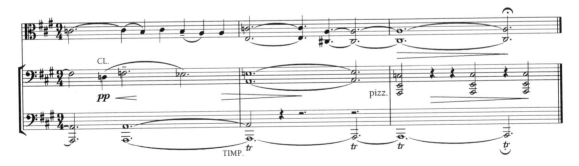

Example 41

Example 42

Example 43

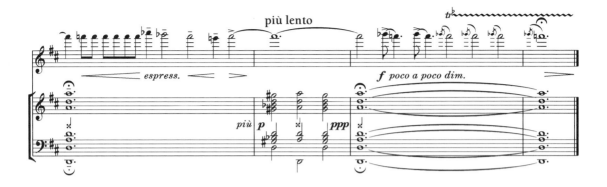

Example 44

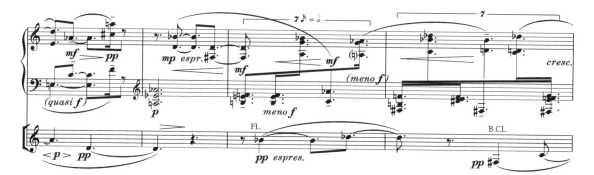

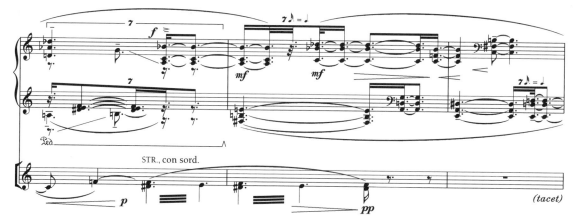

Credits

Illustrations

Plate 1. Andrei Gavrilov and Vladimir Ashkenazy in Moscow, video still from EMI Ldisc ldB 40304-1.

Plate 2. Mstislav Rostropovich.
Courtesy of CORBIS/Hulton-Deutsch Collection.

Plate 3. Artur Rubinstein and Loren Maazel.
Courtesy of CORBIS/Hulton-Deutsch Collection.

Plate 4. Benny Goodman with the Boston Symphony Orchestra.
Courtesy of CORBIS/Bettmann.

Plate 5. Leonard Bernstein in Israel. Courtesy of CORBIS/Bettmann.

Plate 6. Vladimir Horowitz. Courtesy of CORBIS/Bettmann.

Music Examples

Example 40. Piano reduction by Geoffrey Pratley. © Oxford University Press 1930 and 1993. Used by permission.

Example 41. © 1936, 1996 by Universal Edition A.G., Vienna. All rights reserved. Used by permission of European American Music Distribution Corporation, sole U.S. and Canadian agent for Universal Edition A.G., Vienna.

Example 42. © 1940 by Schott Music Universal. All rights reserved. Used by permission of European American Music Distribution Corporation, sole U.S. and Canadian agent for Schott Musik International.

Example 44. Copyright © 1967 (renewed) by Associated Music Publishers Inc. (BMI). International copyright secured. All rights reserved. Reprinted by permission.